St. Lydwine the Virgin

BY

THOMAS À KEMPIS

Canon Regular of the Congregation of Windesheim

TRANSLATION AND INTRODUCTION BY

DOM VINCENT SCULLY, C.R.L.

Author of "Life of the Venerable Thomas à Kempis"

Permissu Superiorum

Nihil obstat.

> FR. INNOCENTIUS APAP, S.Th.M., O.P.
> *Censor Deputatus.*

Imprimatur.

> EDM. CAN. SURMONT,
> *Vic. Gen.*

Westmonasterii,
Die 25 Martii, 1912.

To

ALL PATIENT SUFFERERS

Who share St. Lydwine's expiatory pains
One day to partake of her glory

CONTENTS

	Page
INTRODUCTION.	9
PROLOGUE TO THE FIRST PART	45
CHAPTERS OF THE FIRST PART	49
PROLOGUE TO THE SECOND PART	105
CHAPTERS OF THE SECOND PART.	106

St. Lydwine of Schiedam Virgin

INTRODUCTION

The Life of Lydwine, Virgin, is of all the works of Thomas à Kempis certainly the least original and to English readers generally the least familiar. The latter fact is most probably due to the subject matter. That the work is not original, Thomas himself is our authority, when he states in his *Prologue* that he has read through the "book of the life of the holy and most patient virgin Lydwine," and has now sent it on to his brothers, the Canons Regular of Briel, composed in a style more brief and clear, with certain omissions and his own division of chapters and books. In fact, our venerable Author contented himself with merely editing the biography already published by one John Brugman. A comparison with the latter shows that almost throughout à Kempis has retained even the language of Brugman. This circumstance has rendered the task of translation somewhat ungrateful: but a full compensation has been found in the intense interest which a study of the life itself of this servant of God evoked.

The first sentiment that arises, as one reads the unvarnished and detailed account given by the ancient chroniclers of the appalling sufferings which afflicted Lydwine, may be one of very natural repulsion. But a more attentive consideration of this pathetic figure, lying motionless there in the darkened hovel, enduring the most atrocious pains, with never a murmur of complaint, never a thought of self, embalms the soul with the sweet fragrance of Christian virtue, such a fragrance as refreshed the senses of those who penetrated into her miserable cabin. The thought of the active works of charity, which this victim of expiation initiated and carried out to relieve miseries far less intense than her own, fills the mind with admiration and amazement. And a further contemplation of the marvellous, mystic delights, with which her soul was almost habitually inundated, gives rise to a sense of mingled awe and envy.

It is indeed a wonderful existence to which we are here introduced: on the one hand unexampled physical suffering, wholly unrelieved by natural remedies, wholly unsupported by natural nourishment, and on the other supernatural visitations as unmeasured only as the pains of the poor, tortured, worn-out frame. So marvellous an existence may well excuse a certain amount of previous scepticism, and certainly it is such as to call for proportionate proof. But once that proof is forthcoming, for the scientific and unprejudiced mind there is nothing for it but to accept the facts, be the explanation what it may.

These facts are of two orders. The first regards the sufferings and abstinence of Lydwine. However weird, however varied, however intense, however long continued, and under each and all these heads, however inexplicable from a natural point of view these ailments may be, in themselves they were sensible facts, capable of being observed and tested by all, and by their very strangeness evoking a more close and detailed observation and criticism than would be given to ordinary events of daily life. The same is to be said of her continued and absolute fast. Marvellous and miraculous as is the prolongation of a human life despite such complex and malignant maladies, and despite the absence for so many years of all bodily nourishment and sleep, the only other hypothesis admissible contemplates an alternative far more incredible, viz. that the entire population of a country town —and who does not know the intensity and ingenuity and malevolence of neighbourly curiosity in such centres? —should either have been hoodwinked itself, or should have entered into a vast and meaningless conspiracy to deceive the whole kingdom, princes, medical men, skilled theologians, and strangers of every conceivable quality and degree. The second order of facts regards other favours more directly supernatural. Many of these enter into the same category as the first in so far as they fall immediately under sensible observation. Of the others, as the majority of the raptures and visions recorded, Lydwine herself is our sole authority. If these are to be rejected, it can be only on the supposition that the virgin was suffering from delusion or that she was living a lie: and how far such a theory tallies with the ascertained facts of her character and her conduct may be safely left to the unprejudiced mind to judge.

It would indeed be difficult to find a biography, of which the details, incredible as they may seem at first sight, are presented to us with more convincing authority. The Venerable à Kempis himself was a contemporary of the maiden whose saintly life he undertook to edit; he was born the same year, 1380, and he passed away thirty-eight years after her demise. For some of his facts he quotes the authority of first or second-hand witnesses. For the rest, he has followed very closely John Gerlac and John Brugman; but that, as is sufficiently evident from the *Prologue*, not without considerable deliberation and discussion. Finally, the Author of the *Imitation* was not likely easily to lend the authority of his name to the recounting of unfounded extravagances.

John Brugman, whose *Life* our Author chiefly uses, thus enumerates his sources of information in his *Introduction:* "Let the readers of this biography know that I have received the greater portion of it from the lips of Master John Walters of Lyden: who for nearly eight years was the confessor of that virgin, and learnt these things from her: in part [I have taken it] from the writings of John Gerlac, a certain relative of hers who lived in her house many years: and in part from a letter which the Governors of the city of Schiedam delivered as a testimony of her ailments to Master John Angels of Dordrecht, of the Order of Prémontré, of Marienwaer, who was then Pastor of the town Church: and a little [I have gathered] from the lips of others worthy of faith: but the whole [has been compiled] with the correction or approbation of the aforesaid Master John, the confessor of this virgin, and of John Gerlac." The extract is certainly of interest if only as showing that hagiographers of the fifteenth century were not unaware or careless of the exigencies of historical criticism.

The John Gerlac here mentioned as a relative of the Saint and living many years in her house, was an ascetic writer of some repute and a Canon

Regular of Windesheim, a fervent and humble religious, according to the testimony of his contemporaries. He wrote a biography of his holy kinswoman soon after her death in German, and John Brugman's first *Life*, the one later edited by à Kempis, is little more than a translation into Latin of this.

Subsequently John Brugman wrote another biography with considerably more detail and a good deal of expansion. John Brugman himself was a Friar Minor, a friend of Denys the Carthusian, and he is quoted by Wadding as one of the first preachers of his day, a man remarkable alike for eloquence and sanctity.

Both these biographies are edited and annotated by Papebroch in the Bollandists' *Acta Sanctorum*, April, Vol. II. There also is found a copy of the Letter of the Magistrates of Schiedam, to which John Brugman refers in the extract above, and which he gives *in extenso* in the Prologue to his second *Life*. This curious document seems worthy of a place here, both on account of its own intrinsic interest and as a further witness to the critical investigation to which the actions and sufferings of our

Saint were subjected. The most exacting in these days of boasted research could hardly demand more. A comparison of this Letter with Chapters VI. and VII. of Part 1 of à Kempis' *Life* will show that he, as well as Brugman before him, made free use of this authentic piece. The reader must forgive the involved phraseology for the sake of a literal translation.

"We, the Baillif,[1] the Mayor,[2] the Bourgmaestres, Sheriffs and Councillors of the town of Schiedam, in the Duchy of Holland, in the Diocese of Utrecht, make known to all that we have seen and read, in the year of the Lord 1421 on the twelfth day of September, the Letter sealed with the seal of our town, containing word for word as follows:

"To the faithful of Christ, all and sundry, spiritual and lay, adults and minors, nobles and commoners, to men and persons of both sexes of whatever state, rank or condition they may be, within cities or without, on land or on sea, or wheresoever they may tarry, or have their home or place of habitation,

---
[1] Appointed by the Prince.
[2] Elected by the people.

whom the present letters may reach, the Baillif, the Mayor, the Bourgmaestres, Sheriffs and Councillors of the town of Schiedam, in the Duchy of Holland, in the Diocese of Utrecht, greeting with ever humble salutation and witness to the truth. Whereas right reason judges, justice demands and requires that true happenings and cases may be openly published, reported and manifested, yea ought justly to be published, reported and manifested; especially those wherein the praise, honour and glory of God may be present and shine forth.

Therefore we certify and we make known, and we desire the faithful of Christ aforesaid all and sundry to know, we publish, we report, and we witness in truth to these writings, concerning the facts and events most wondrous and strange, which in the abovenamed our city have happened and taken place, and still daily take place and happen in a certain virgin, named Liedwy Peters.[1] Be this known that the said virgin and maid was grievously sick, and very greatly tormented in her bed, whereon

[1] *i.e.* Liedwy (daughter) of Peter: her father was called Peter, his surname Johns, *i.e.* of John, after his father, who was a John Peters.

ST. LYDWINE *of* SCHIEDAM

also she lies and has lain well twenty-three years on the Feast of the Purification of the Blessed Virgin Mary last passed. And within the same time she has never taken or received save one half a pint of wine a week or thereabouts, with a little water, or a little sugar, or a very little cinnamon well ground; except that within the first three years of her ailment, occasionally and between times, she took a small piece of apple or bread, and sometimes ate or drank a little fresh milk: but within the seven years last passed she has used no food or drink at all, nor does use any at present.

"She does not sleep, nor for all the above-written seven years has she ever slept, except very little, and scarcely for the space of two nights, all reckoned together. And she lies now so pitiably and miserably, that she has lost her intestines and is deprived of the same. And grey worms, full of water of the same colour, thick as a spindle-end, about as long as the joint of a finger, eat and gnaw her flesh, without any fetor or ill odour arising thence, (the which we write with the leave and reverence of all). And when in times

ST. LYDWINE *of* SCHIEDAM

past she was wont to be moved or handled, then it was necessary to bind her body well above about the shoulders with bandages, or with a towel, or with some such thing: otherwise the whole body would have fallen into small portions and would have utterly dropped to pieces. But now in later times she cannot in any way be moved, nor could she be within the seven years last passed, during which she has lain and still lies on her back, and cannot move save her head and one arm.[1]

"And sometimes at intervals from her mouth, nose, ears and other passages she sends forth much blood, notwithstanding that she takes no food or drink, nor has taken save as above described. And the same virgin and maid within the same seven years aforesaid had and still has every third day a great and grievous tertian fever, which first comes to her with an unutterable heat: and not long after this comes a terrible cold: and then again heat and cold by turn.

---

[1] It seems that the right arm was quite withered and shrunken, holding to the body by a single nerve, the consequence of an attack of that strange and terrible malady of the Middle Ages, known as the *Sacred Fire*, or *St. Anthony's Fire.*

And this lasted thus for well half a year: but after this period she has cold enduring for a time and then heat. And when she is freed from this fever, then is she quite unconscious for ten or twelve hours. And when she has and suffers the aforesaid fevers, then she vomits or sends out by the mouth at night much red water, so that a quart vessel is filled thereof in a week: and moreover in addition within the year she also vomits and throws up well two measures full of this water

"The aforesaid virgin and maid has also in her body three openings: of which each is well as large as the inner hollow or bottom of a common cup, and they are as black as pitch, as appears to those who look in and see. And from one of them, which is in the stomach of that virgin and maid, there run and overflow at intervals as many sometimes as two hundred together of the aforesaid worms; and upon it is placed a kind of plaster mixed and made of honey and fresh flour of the best wheat: and therefrom those worms suck and take their nourishment, otherwise they would torment her even to death: and if this flour were old and not fresh, those worms would not have such, or use that plaster. All these things have been proved and found thus by experience: and now those openings are closed.

"Every fortnight also the above-named virgin and maid receives the most holy and venerable sacrament of the altar, the Eucharist; and the priest who communicates her must needs use skill and care when he communicates her: otherwise she could not receive or swallow the Eucharist. And then he gives her very little water: which also she cannot very well pass, or swallow, but first she works it in her throat for a time, as one who gargles; and sometimes he gives her no water on account of the difficulty of passing or receiving the same.[1] Moreover, this virgin and maid from below even to the stomach is utterly and wholly putrefied; and it is needful to close this wound with a little cushion of wool made especially for the purpose, about the size of a fist: otherwise her intestines and lower parts would quite fall away. And thus in truth the marvels and portents, which in the said

[1] This giving of a little water after the Communion of the sick is in accordance with a prescription of the Roman Ritual.

virgin and maid have been wrought and are still daily wrought, are exceedingly great and so numerous and varied, that they cannot be clearly and fully written, or described by the pen. The oft-named virgin and maid was also fourteen years of age, when her ailment first overtook and befell her.

"And whereas we, the Baillif, the Mayor, the Bourgmaestres, Sheriffs and Councillors aforesaid have been well and fully informed and certified of the above written details, yea daily well perceive and witness them: therefore we seal the present letters for a plain and true testimony, with our seal which we use for cases, appended in the year of the Lord, 1421, on the eve of the Blessed Mary Magdalene, the twenty-first day of the month of July."

In common with the hagiographers of his time, our Author does not follow the chronological order in his *Life*. Moreover, he gives us very few dates. The same negligence is observable in other details, as for instance in the names of personages who figure in the story. In fact, he wrote simply for the edification of his brothers in religion, and for this purpose doubtless he considered such items superfluous, even when he did not regard them as already known. Nevertheless he had a very definite scheme of his own in the arrangement of books and chapters. In the First Book he narrates, and that in a roughly consecutive order, an account of the progress and variety of Lydwine's physical sufferings, and a history of her corporal works of mercy, together with the miraculous favours whereby God showed His appreciation of her charity. The mention of her poverty leads him to speak of the spirit of poverty and other virtues, and of the death of her father. This induces him to digress further and dwell on the good qualities of her grandfather, and finally of the passing away of her mother. Moreover, it must not be forgotten that these successive bereavements were a part and a very sensible part of the afflictions of the saint; for she was tenderly attached to the members of her family, and one after another she saw them taken away from her. The Author returns to this subject also in the Second Book. This Second Book treats more directly of the inner, spiritual life of the Saint, and of the prodigious graces of which she was finally the object. Here again he roughly outlines the progress from the innocence, not free from thoughtlessness and other faults, of childhood to the ripe perfection attained after long years of patient suffering and almost uninterrupted union with God. The three miracles, with which he fittingly closes his history, he received, as he tells us himself, directly from Dr. William Sonderdank, an eyewitness and a medical man.

As, however, it may assist the modern reader to a better appreciation of the affecting story of this servant of God to have an idea of the chronological sequence of events, I give here a brief epitome of the biography, arranged according to the few dates which à Kempis and Brugman have supplied.

1380. The Saint's mother is painlessly delivered of a daughter during the singing of the Passion, Palm Sunday, March 18th.

1380–1394. Lydwine passes a bright childhood in a poor, but very Christian household, and is remarked for her piety and other rich gifts both of nature and grace. Her father receives on her behalf some very advantageous offers of marriage, but the child declares her intention of remaining always a maid. About her fourteenth year she is stricken with illness, and then, before she is quite recovered, she receives a fatal fall upon the ice, February 2nd, 1394.

1394-1397. These three years are a sad period of material and spiritual neglect. One malady succeeds another: the child suffers and frets. At this time she receives Holy Communion once a year, at Easter-tide, when she is carried to the Church for the purpose. However, the miracle narrated in Chapter V. shows that even then the maid must have been possessed of remarkable purity and singleness of purpose.

1398. About this time her confessor, John Pot, taught the invalid how to meditate upon the Passion of Christ. This she finds very difficult at first, but with persevering efforts and especially with the grace brought by a fervent Communion, she acquires great recollection, and now begins to feel happiness in her pains, recognising therein God's will and her special vocation. At the same time the Confessor commences to communicate her twice a year.

ST. LYDWINE *of* SCHIEDAM

1400. Lydwine took to her bed, never again to touch the earth in life or after death.

1402. About this date Lydwine's mother, Petronilla, died. This event marks a real epoch in the Saint's life, for, having generously ceded all her merits to her dying mother, she now regarded herself as under a necessity to compensate for this loss by renewed efforts and redoubled penance.

1405. It was about this time that the Saint commenced that series of wonderful ecstasies, which were to continue with but few interruptions until her death.

1406 is marked as a year of a very severe winter, during which Lydwine suffered indescribably from the cold.

1413. About this time commences Lydwine's complete fast from all food save the Holy Eucharist, although indeed hitherto her nourishment had been so scanty as scarcely to deserve the name. From the same epoch dates her entire freedom from sleep.

1421. This is the date of the magisterial inquiry, the result of which has been given above. In this document her confessor is mentioned as com-

ST. LYDWINE *of* SCHIEDAM

municating her once a fortnight. But henceforth until her death she received habitually in the intervals of two days between her quartan fevers.

1423 is the date of the death of her brother William, over which Lydwine grieved so intensely as to be deprived for some time of her wonted spiritual consolations.

1425. The sufferings endured by Lydwine at the hands of the Duke of Burgundy's mercenaries merit for her a martyr's crown.

1426 witnesses the death of the Saint's beloved niece Petronilla, and therewith the snapping of the final cord of an affection, which, however pure and blameless, was not entirely for her Divine Spouse.

1433. April 14th, the Saint's happy death.

1434. A chapel is built in the cemetery by her tomb.

A few words now to bring the story of our Saint to the present day.

In accordance with her own wish Lydwine's house was transformed into a hospital, or home for aged females, by Dr. William Sonderdank, a physician remarkable for his piety and generosity, and devotion to the holy maid.[1] It seems that this hospice was placed in the charge of Franciscan nuns; for Molanus says that these Sisters had a convent on the spot, with a chapel and altar in the very bedchamber of the virgin. "But," he adds, "the enemies of the Faith and of all piety utterly destroyed all this in the year [15]72." The destruction, however, does not appear to have extended to the building itself, for this was used as an orphanage again in 1605, and was rebuilt in 1771.

To prevent the profanation of the Saint's relics during the religious troubles of the sixteenth century, the Catholic party under the Archduchess Isabelle and Prince Albert bought Lydwine's mortal remains from the Reformers, 1615, and translated them to Brussels, where Matthias, Archbishop of Mechlin and Primate of Belgium, after due authentication, authorised their veneration, granting to the same effect an indulgence of forty days. A copy of the Metropolitan's Act, dated Jan. 14th, 1616, is to be found in the Bollandists, *loc. cit.*

The same year, 1616, the Archduchess

[1] See *Note*, page 211.

made a present of a portion of the holy relics to the Canonesses Regular of Mons, in Hainult, on the occasion of a plague which was devastating that city. Ten years later a further and very considerable portion of the relics was bestowed by the same Princess on the Carmelite Nuns of Brussels, whose convent she had founded in 1606. Finally, at Isabelle's death, the remainder of the relics were transferred with great pomp to St. Gudule's, the Cathedral Church of Brussels.

The official documents concerning all these translations and of these various marks of public honour paid to the relics were happily never lost—an exact copy is given in the Bollandists—and thus it came to pass that when within the last fifty years advances were made at Rome to obtain Papal recognition and approbation of the veneration of the faithful to the holy maid Lydwine, there was no difficulty in proving the fact of the *cultus ab immemorabili tempore.*

It was on the strength of this immemorial cultus that, after all the tedious process and scrupulous details wherewith such grave matters are ever regulated in the Eternal City, Pope Leo XIII issued a short Decree, dated March 14th, 1890, solemnly approving the veneration paid to the virgin Lydwine under the title of Blessed, or Saint. At the same time an Office and Mass of the Saint were approved for the Diocese of Harlem; and the Carmelites of Brussels were requested to bestow a portion of her relics on the Church of Our Lady of the Visitation, Schiedam, one of the three Churches, which to-day minister to the spiritual needs of the ten thousand Catholics who now dwell in St. Lydwine's native town.

It was there that the present writer had the happiness of seeing and venerating the holy relics, in the July of 1906. Ever since I had taken up the study of the life and times of the Venerable Thomas à Kempis, I had longed to pay a visit to the scenes amid which his days were passed. I read with intense interest the graphic account of such a visit given by Sir Francis Cruise in his *Thomas à Kempis* (Kegan Paul & Co., 1887), and I promised myself that if the opportunity should be mine, I also would pass over the same holy ground. The opportunity presented itself in 1906 and pocketing Dr. Cruise's work as my

Baedeker, and a more reliable guide could not be desired, I made a little à Kempis pilgrimage by way of Kempen, Deventer, Zwolle, this last of course including Agnetenberg and Windesheim, and finally, in the interests of the present volume, Schiedam.

With regard to my visit to the first three named towns there is little to add to what has been already so well described in the treatise just cited. I note merely that at Kempen, the oil painting of the Venerable Thomas, which Sir Francis Cruise found in the old Franciscan Church, now hangs in the Study Hall of the splendid Collegium Thommaeum, a *Convictus* or Boarding House for scholars from a distance who attend the courses in the fine Grammar School opposite. Likewise the portrait formerly hung in the Town Hall is now preserved in the Kempen Museum, together with another portrait and several engravings and editions of à Kempis. In the Grammar School Library there is a fine à Kempis collection, the initiative of which is due to Dr. Pohl, the painstaking Editor of the new critical issue of the *Omnia Opera*, from which the present translation is taken.

Finally, since the date of Dr. Cruise's visit, there has been erected in the close of the Parish Church, and within view of the site of the birthplace of à Kempis, a magnificent statue in bronze, on a massive pedestal in black marble, representing our venerable Author in the habit of a Canon Regular, seated with a volume of the *Imitation* open in one hand and a pen in the other. On the front of the pedestal is engraved: Thomas von Kempen. On the back the words in Dutch: Raised by the Thomas Institute to the great son of Kempen, 1901. On Thomas' left the verses from the *Imitation*, book iv (iii) ch. 1: "Happy the soul that heareth the Lord speaking within her; and from His mouth receiveth a word of consolation. Happy the ears that receive the accents of the divine whisper, and take no notice of the whisperings of the world." On the other side, the further quotation: "If thou didst know the whole Bible by heart and the sayings of all the philosophers, what would it all profit thee without the love of God and His grace? Vanity of vanity, and all is vanity, save loving God and serving Him alone." It is really a striking and most impressive monument, and one cannot but rejoice that the Venerable Thomas is thus remembered and honoured in his native town.

At Deventer I found things exactly as described by Sir Francis Cruise. There I had the consolation of gazing upon the skulls of Gerard Groote and Florentius Radewyn, which having been rescued from the old Parish Church in the time of the Reformation riots, are now reverently preserved in the sacristy of the Broedern Kirk. If I may add a personal note, I must say that I can never forget the intelligent courtesy and homely kindness of the Sacristan, or Koster, of this church. Indeed throughout my pilgrimage I met with the same consideration on all sides, which was in truth the more welcome, as "greatly daring" I had undertaken this tour alone and quite unconversant with either German or Dutch.

The interest of the pilgrimage culminated at Zwolle, in which district the Venerable à Kempis passed by far the greater portion of his long, laborious career. But here also everything has been so thoroughly described before me by my friend, Dr. Cruise, that once more

I must content myself with referring the reader to his interesting pages. Since his date, however, a magnificent monument has been erected in the Church of St. Michael to enshrine the relics of à Kempis. This is minutely described in my *Life of the Ven. Thomas à Kempis*, (Washbourne, 1901); and I need not go over that ground again. There has been some talk recently of founding an à Kempis Museum in Zwolle, which is, by the way, one of the neatest and prettiest little towns I have ever seen. While awaiting funds and a suitable locality for this purpose, two valuable portraits and many other items of interest are preserved in the central hall of an ancient hospice for the aged, named Emmanuel Huis; these were shown me with the utmost courtesy by M. Th. Heerkens, of Zwolle, a prominent member of the Upper Chamber of the States-General and an ardent à Kempist. Finally, there is a movement on foot to erect a statue to the Ven. Thomas in the public square of the town.

On my visit to Windesheim I was kindly accompanied by the Rev. B. M. Brom, Curate of St. Michael's, Niewstraat. Of the famous Canonry nothing remains, save part of the Infirmary, now used as the Protestant temple of the little village. Let into the wall of this chapel are two tombstones, one with the recumbent figure of a priest, with chalice, &c., and an almost illegible inscription deciphered by F. Haefer, President of the Society of Thomas à Kempis, and furnished me by Fr. Brom, as follows: (*Hic jacent*) *venerabiles et devoti viri Theodorus de Herxen et dominus* (*Gerardus Scatte de Calkar*).

I come now to the last stage of my pilgrimage, and that which more directly concerns the present volume, Schiedam, the native town of St. Lydwine. Here I parted company with my genial guide, Sir Francis Cruise, but I knew that another, J.-K. Huysmans, had been here also before me.[1]

The first object of my inquiry was the Church of the Visitation, where, as related above, the relics of St. Lydwine are preserved. I called upon the Pastor and explained the motive of my visit, expressing at the same time a desire to celebrate holy Mass at the shrine of the

[1] See his very original and intensely interesting *Sainte Lydwine de Schiedam*. Paris: Stock.

Saint. Unfortunately, this privilege was just then impracticable: the Church was undergoing one of those thorough "spring cleanings" of which the good Hollanders are so prodigal, and one altar only was available for the holy Sacrifice. The Pastor, however, consoled me by promising to have the relics exposed for my veneration on the morrow. He was as good as his word, and the next morning I had the happiness of praying before the exposed relics of the holy maid, whom I had learnt to reverence and love, as I unravelled the story of her sufferings, virtues, and rewards from the quaint Latin of à Kempis.

The relics are enshrined in a very fine altar, constructed in an exquisite little chapel off the south aisle. In bas-relief over the centre stands a figure of the Saint, holding a crucifix, and before her an Angel presenting her the traditional rose-branch.[1] On the right hand of the reliquary is another bas-relief, representing Our Divine Saviour, attended by Angels and Saints, administering the last rites to the dying virgin:[2] on the left, the Saint, as found by her neigh-

See *Note*, page 191.   [2] See *Note*, page 190.

bours immediately after death, her hands joined upon her breast, all traces of long years of disease banished, all and more than all her youthful freshness and beauty restored.[1] Below, occupying the whole length of the altar, the Saint reclining, earnestly studying her crucifix, the Angel hovering near with the rose-branch.

Round the walls of the Chapel are depicted, with considerable verve and skill, seven epochs from the life of the Saint. The Statue of Our Lady of Schiedam smiles upon her in her childhood (*Part I, chap. ii*). The fateful fall on the ice (*Part I, chap. iv*). John Pot earnestly exhorts the sick maid to essay meditation upon the Passion of Christ (*Part II, chap. i*). The Miraculous Host (*Part II, chap. xxii*). Her ecstatic voyage to the Holy Land and vision of the Passion (*Part II, chap. ii*). The multiplication of bread, meat and money given in alms (*Part I, chaps. xx, xxii*). The brutal assault of the mercenaries of Picardy, in which an Angel is seen hovering above the Saint, holding ready a martyr's crown (*Part II, chap. vii*).

[1] Part II, chaps. xxvii, xxviii.

Finally, the fire of Schiedam, where Angels again appear protecting the Saint (*Part II, chaps. v, xvi*).

Anent this last incident, it is worthy of note that the Saint is regarded by all, Catholics and Protestants alike, as the Guardian of the town against fire. It is certainly a remarkable fact that since her death no more than a single house has been burnt at a time, a significant record considering the inflammable material stored in such abundance in this town, known the world over for its Hollands, or Schiedam schnapps.

After I had duly noted these various points, the good Pastor further devoted a considerable portion of his much occupied time in showing me from the Parish Archives a collection of various documents, ancient and modern, connected with the history of the Saint and especially with the process of her recent canonization. It is not necessary to go into these details here: they would be more in place in a full and modern English life, such as that already quoted of J.-K. Huysmans in French, or that other which M. l'Abbé Cordurier so charmingly composed for the comfort and edification of his "dear incurables of the Hospital of Bourg."[1] What chiefly interested me at the time was an old Dutch translation of à Kempis' *Life* of the Saint, and a series of twenty-two quaint little woodcuts, depicting various incidents from her story.

The Curé also informed me that devotion to St. Lydwine is very popular in the town, and that in his Church there is a special service in her honour every Thursday evening, for which is used a manual of prayers compiled for the purpose by his predecessor. I noticed statues of the Saint in the two other Catholic Churches of Schiedam, served by Dominicans, who in fact ministered to the spiritual needs of this district even through the Reformation days.

One other most interesting relic I was also conducted to see, the ancient marble slab which formerly covered the Saint's tomb. This, it is said, was placed face down—the figure of the Saint is sculptured thereon—in the pavement of the now Protestant Church to prevent Catholics coming to pay their devotions to it. Another account asserts that Protestants themselves out of respect

[1] *Vie de la Bienheureuse Lidwine, Vierge, Modele des Malades et des Infirmes.* Paris: Retaux.

would walk round rather than tread upon it. Be that as it may, one dark night the precious slab disappeared from its dishonoured resting-place. Through inability or connivance the authorities made no active pursuit. And now the stone with its figure and its inscription, giving the date of Lydwine's death in old Dutch, may be seen in the tiny Chapel of the Dominican convent, close to the Church of the Visitation. While I was examining it there, the old ladies who are tended and sheltered by the gentle Sisters in their destitution or infirmity, dropped in one by one to pay their visit or tell their beads, and the thought passed through my mind how pleased St. Lydwine must be that this relic should be preserved in a Christian home for the poor and aged, such as she had destined her own house to be.

I visited also the ancient parish Church of St. John the Baptist, rebuilt after the fire in St. Lydwine's own days, and for so long the resting-place of her holy remains. On my way I noted a gay wedding party issue from the portals of the Town Hall, and this incident, in contrast with the utter void of the huge empty white-washed building of St.

John's—its whole furniture the bare wooden benches ranged round the organ and reading desks—seemed to me a striking illustration of the sad changes wrought by the religious revolt of the sixteenth century.

It is round this venerable Church that what remains of ancient Schiedam still survives, and as I wandered about amid its narrow streets, quaint bulging buildings, frequent canals and wooden drawbridges, it was not so difficult for the imagination to people and animate the scene again with the personages and incidents of the Life of St. Lydwine.

But, for the rest, it is well understood that Schiedam is not a town of which Dutchmen boast, or to which tourists crowd. Its staple industry is gin, and the whole atmosphere is impregnated with the odour of the boiling grain used in the manufacture; and were it not for the redeeming native virtue, this town alone of all that I had seen in the Netherlands would be positively dirty.

To conclude, the text, on which the following translation is based, is that of Dr. Pohl, edited from the autograph of à Kempis, which is preserved in the University Library, Louvain. There the original may be seen bound in one volume with Thomas' *Sermons to the Novices Regular*,[1] the caligraphy still beautifully clear and legible.

The footnotes throughout are the Translator's.

St. Ives, Cornwall,
  All Hallows, 1910.

[1] *Translation.* London : Kegan Paul. 1910.

Life of Lydwine, Virgin
Part I

LIFE OF LYDWINE, VIRGIN

PART I

PROLOGUE TO THE LIFE OF LYDWINE, VIRGIN

To the Religious Brethren, Canons Regular of the monastery of St. Elizabeth, near Briel in the country of Zeeland. Brother N., a poor pilgrim, humbly begging the suffrages of your prayers. Most beloved brothers in Christ, since we profess the same Order and Rule, it is just that according to the saying of St. James the Apostle we pray for one another, and adorn our faith with good works, and keep the bond of charity in true love. May your fraternity then deign to know that at the request of your brethren I have read through the book[1] of the life of the

---

[1] Brugman's first *Life*, founded chiefly on John Gerlac's German MS. See *Introduction*.

ST. LYDWINE *of* SCHIEDAM

holy and most patient virgin Lydwine: and as you have long desired I now out of charity send you the same to read composed in a style more brief and clear. Do not take it ill that I have delayed; nor attribute to presumption what I have done: because the counsel of your venerable Prior came and urged me to the doing. For what seemed at first difficult to me, by the help of God through your prayers has at length arrived at completion. I have divided the whole matter of the book into two parts, and to each part I have prefixed its own chapters. Also by the advice of certain religious I have omitted many things which seemed liable maybe to cause doubt or nice questioning to some simple souls. I have chosen therefore from many things to write and gather rather those which might instruct in virtue and clearly show a way of humble imitation to those who should read. But they are almost all fit subject for wonder, surpassing my experience; and I leave the judgment of them to my betters. But I trust that the prayers of the humble will be more pleasing and acceptable to God and the holy virgin herself, than to search into lofty things, and foolishly gossip of the secrets of God. Let it not disturb anyone if the name is spelt sometimes Lydia or Lydwine, for this is found in other histories of the saints: as Agna is suitably written for Agnes, Walburga for Walburgis. We read of a Lydia in the *Acts*[1] of the Apostles, whom Paul the Apostle converted, and in whose house he received hospitality; and our Lydia willingly received many religious to discourse of things divine: and taught by a holy angel she very often brought the grace of heavenly comfort to the troubled of heart.

[1] Acts xv 14, 15.

THE CHAPTERS OF THE FIRST PART OF THIS BOOK OF THE LIFE OF LYDWINE, VIRGIN

Chap.		Page
I.	Of the birthplace and birth of the virgin Lydwine, and the probity of her parents	51
II.	Of her devotion to the image of the Blessed Virgin	54
III.	Of her strong purpose in the state of virginity	56
IV.	Of the beginning of her weakness, and the occasion of her long illness	58
V.	Of the opinion of a certain doctor, and the miracle that befell her	60
VI.	Of the scantiness of her nourishment for many years	63
VII.	Of the various illnesses and pains that tormented her day and night	65
VIII.	Of the severity of her fever, and a fresh disease in her leg	70
IX.	Of the hardness of her bed, and the cold she suffered in winter	73
X.	Of her watchings and struggle against sleep	76

CONTENTS

Chap.		Page
XI.	Of the poverty and endurance of her father	79
XII.	Of the illusion of Satan who cast her father into a ditch	81
XIII.	Of the death of her father on the vigil of the Conception of the Blessed Virgin Mary	83
XIV.	Of the death of John Peters her grandfather, and his long continence	85
XV.	Of the death of Petronilla her mother	87
XVI.	Of her state after her mother's death, and her pity for the poor	89
XVII.	Of the burning of her bed, which she put out with one hand without any injury	90
XVIII.	Of the ashes ministered to her by an angel at the beginning of Lent	91
XIX.	Of the wine miraculously placed in her cup	93
XX.	Of the money paid for her brother, and multiplied in her purse	95
XXI.	Of the ham given to the poor, and miraculously replaced by another	97
XXII.	Of the meat and peas given to the poor, and multiplied	99
XXIII.	Of the vision of a heavenly table, filled by the alms of the poor	101

CHAPTER I

OF THE BIRTHPLACE AND BIRTH OF THE VIRGIN LYDWINE, AND THE PROBITY OF HER PARENTS

On the western coast of Holland is situated a certain city called from a neighbouring stream [1] Schiedam, which God, Who is mighty and wonderful in His saints, adorned with the wondrous and unexampled patience of a certain holy virgin. This virgin was rightly called in effect and name from her much suffering Lydwine; [2] because, scourged by divers sicknesses, she became most pleasing to her heavenly Spouse Christ. By the lovers of the world, while she lived, she was deemed poor and mean; but by the Creator of Heaven she was chosen as a most precious pearl out of the waves of the sea, and in the heavenly kingdom placed most high with the holy virgins. Her origin was noble from a military family; but it was made more

[1] The Schie.   [2] *Lyden*, to suffer.

noble and illustrious by the grace of the Holy Ghost coming upon her. Her father was called Peter; who, although he was noble of lineage according to the dignity of the world, nevertheless by the permission of God he had come down to such poverty that in the time of Duke William, the son of Albert Duke in the County of Holland, he sought food and the necessaries of life by keeping the night watches of the city; whereby to support himself and his family decently. This Peter, when after the manner usual with men in the world he had earned his livelihood in simplicity in much toil for some years, took to wife one Petronilla, a woman of great probity and virtue, befitting his name and nobility; who by the gift of God flourished with the seed of many children, and, fearing God, strove to rule her house religiously. She begot eight sons, and one daughter named Lydwine, whom certain Latinists call Lydia, concerning whom the present discourse intends to relate the many marvels which God wrought by her before many witnesses. Although, therefore, being the mother of so many children she had suffered the greatest labour in the birth of each, nevertheless in the bringing forth of this daughter she felt almost no pain. For having entered the Church on Palm Sunday, feeling that the time of her childbirth was at hand, with speed she returned home; and almost without any great pain she brought forth this child of election during the reading of the Lord's Passion, in the year of the Lord's Incarnation, one thousand three hundred and eighty,[1] on the fifteenth of the Kalends of April[2] on the morrow of Gertrude Virgin,[3] in the time of Pope Urban the Sixth, the third year of his pontificate, the reverend prelate Florentius, dear both to the clergy and the whole people, sitting in the See of lower Utrecht. This daughter then, having been born in the fifth place in the order of children, and regenerated in the baptism of Christ, received the name of Lydwine, or Lydia,

[1] The year which also witnessed the birth of the Venerable à Kempis himself.

[2] March 18th.

[3] St. Gertrude of Nivelles, daughter of Pepin of Landen, Duke of Brabant and ancestor of Charlemagne. Her feast is kept in the Lowlands on March 18th. This Saint must not be confounded with the Benedictine St. Gertrude, whose feast falls Nov. 15th.

given her by her parents. She was truly an ornament among the daughters of men and a mirror of modesty; but by the ordinance of God from eternity she soon became a devout contemplator of the Lord's Passion and conformed to the crucified by many wounds of bodily sickness.

CHAPTER II

OF HER DEVOTION TO THE IMAGE OF THE BLESSED VIRGIN

When this maiden, then, was seven or eight years of age, by the inspiration of God she commenced to have a great devotion to the image of the blessed Virgin Mary, which stood in the church of Schiedam. The townsmen of that city relate that this statue was obtained very miraculously and bought for a small sum from a certain man, the sculptor of the said image. For when he, wishing to go to the fair at Antwerp and sell the image there at a better price, had gone on board ship, taking the image with him, the image became of such a great weight that twenty or more men

ST. LYDWINE *of* SCHIEDAM

could not move the boat from the shore. Seeing this, the seamen in amaze considered that the difficulty of moving the vessel came from the presence of the image, and that it wished to have the place of its dwelling there. After a brief counsel, then, the artist sold the image to the citizens, who for reverence set aside a special choir to it in the church. And later in honour of the blessed and glorious Mary ever a Virgin many of the townspeople of both sexes associating together instituted a certain confraternity. And this image was of wood and so light that one man could easily have borne it. This image therefore the young maiden, when she had carried their dinner to her two brothers who went to school, before she returned home, entering the church, lovingly visited; and she devoutly strove to honour the same as best she could by the angelic salutation. And this good and praiseworthy beginning indeed was remarkable in her childish days, and it was a presage of greater grace in the future, from the years of her youth even to the end of her life. When therefore she was reproached by her mother for her late return, the dove without gall replied, that she had entered the church to greet the blessed Virgin, and that she in turn had smiled upon her. Hearing which her mother was satisfied, and gently contented ceased to trouble her. For she was a dear and only daughter; and she was found worthily engaged in the work of God and the praise of the blessed Virgin, and was not therefore to be restrained from her devotion.

CHAPTER III

OF HER STRONG PURPOSE IN THE STATE OF VIRGINITY

Having passed the years of infancy, when she was now advancing in the age of girlhood, she was endowed with such beauty of body and quickness of mind and other gifts of nature bestowed on her by God, that when she was twelve years old she was sought by many in marriage. To the which her father exhorted her; the mother would by no means agree because of her ignorance and youth, but rather dissuading, asked him not to disturb her. Then she with constancy answered her father, that he would never induce her to this ; yea, that if there were no other means of escape she would treat herself in such wise that no one would seek her in wedlock. Wherefore she daily besought the Lord that He would take all harmful and fleshly love away from her heart, that she might be able to love Him alone, her God and Lord, with pure heart and body. Whose prayers and desires the loving and merciful Lord heard without delay, Who had chosen her from eternity a spouse unto Himself; and providing by a wondrous dispensation, He accomplished her will in much bodily suffering, according to that saying of His holy word. " Every branch that beareth fruit My Father will purge it ; that it may bring forth more fruit" (John xv 2). For the earth was good, producing the flowers of modesty; but lest the vanities of the world or the delights of the flesh should violate the seal of virginity, Christ hedged it round with thorns and most grievous pains, that it might not be fit for any nuptial bed.

ST. LYDWINE *of* SCHIEDAM

CHAPTER IV

OF THE BEGINNING OF HER WEAKNESS, AND THE OCCASION OF HER LONG ILLNESS

When therefore she was in her fifteenth year, lest she might begin to wander after the flocks of her worldly companions,[1] the physician of souls, Christ, lovingly visited her for the salvation of her soul and fettered her with a certain bodily weakness, from which afterwards she partially recovered. It happened then at the end of the fifteenth year of her age about the feast of the Purification of the blessed Virgin Mary,[2] that she was invited by her girl companions to go with them upon the ice shod with skates; when one of her comrades going along over the ice at a rapid pace, and unable to stop herself, caught Lydia by the hand; and before long she suddenly fell upon some fragments of ice, and, seriously hurt, broke a small rib in her right side. From which fracture many pains befell her, and increased. For first a hard abscess grew round the place of the broken rib; and although her

---

[1] A reference to *Canticles* i 6.   [2] Feb. 2nd.

parents expended much to heal it, nevertheless they were not able to obtain the wished for cure. And when no one could heal her, and she had been frequently moved from place to place, from bed to bed, as the violence of her disease demanded; at length in the sixteenth year of her age, on the vigil of St. John Baptist,[1] when her father had come to her to console her, she, starting up from the place where she lay, in her weakness fell doubled up upon the knees of her father. And in this brusque movement the abscess was broken, and the matter flowed in abundance through her mouth with vomiting; and thereupon she became so feeble that she was thought to be almost dead. From that time forward she now began to be afflicted with constant infirmities, in which, before she had the taste of things spiritual, she accepted human and bodily remedies, as need required; although they profited but little, and did not relieve her pain. And so for the first three years of her sickness at Eastertide she was taken or carried to the church for Holy Communion; and as she could not stand or walk upon her feet she used a stick

[1] June 23rd.

or a crutch, creeping along inside or out of doors. Often also she drank copiously of the cold water of the ditch, although it was muddy; or, coming to the fire, she would take it hot or warm from the saucepans, which nevertheless she immediately threw up from her weakened stomach. For want then of human counsel, and with an increase of careless management, her body wasted away; but the soul in its vessel of clay was preserved by a hidden grace for great merit hereafter, that in her might be accomplished what is read of blessed Job. "Behold, Satan, he is in thy hand: but yet save his life" (Job ii 6).

CHAPTER V

OF THE OPINION OF A CERTAIN DOCTOR, AND THE MIRACLE THAT BEFELL HER

A certain doctor from Delft, Master Andrew by name,[1] visiting her, told her

[1] The author has here followed John Brugman in his *Life* translated from Gerlac: but in his later and corrected work Brugman attributes these remarks to Godfrey of Hague, who is mentioned in ch. iii, and whose son, also a doctor, appears in Book II.

parents as in prophecy, that by no means would she obtain health, even if they should expend a large sum of English nobles for her. The same experienced Master, to console her parents and kinsfolk, also added that God would work such and so great supernatural wonders in her, that for a weight of gold the size of the maiden's head he would wish that she were his daughter: for from such an offspring he would hope to receive the greatest joy.

And there befell, in the aforesaid three years while the maiden was lying abed ill, a thing very miraculous, which God deigned to manifest to the glory of His name and to make known the virgin's merit. Two men in the city excited in mind against one another began to quarrel, and one pursued the other with a drawn sword to strike and wound, or kill him. The other of them therefore in terror fled to the house and chamber of this maiden, that hiding there he might escape the hands of his pursuer. Whom the other following soon after, asked of her mother Petronilla whether he had entered the house. And she, wishing to save the fugitive by her lie and to hinder the pursuer from shedding blood, answered him that he had not entered. But he, not believing the words of the mother, went into the inner room of the sick girl. And when he had asked her whether he had entered her chamber, the holy virgin with hope in God confidently replied in the affirmative. At which answer her mother, being angry, gave her daughter a blow, as if she had added to her misery the treason of malice by her incautious words. Then the daughter replied to the mother with constancy: "I therefore told the truth, because I hoped that the truth would conceal him who fled to it." Which also happened, by the providence of God. For he who was sought unto death stood before the eyes of his pursuer, and was quite unseen. He departed therefore, giving over the pursuit of the fugitive, not knowing that the power of God had been there. Seeing which, her mother extolled the faith of her daughter far exalted above her faith, or rather her want of faith; and henceforth she conceived a fuller love towards her, and began to bear her infirmities more kindly.

CHAPTER VI

OF THE SCANTINESS OF HER NOURISHMENT FOR MANY YEARS

After this her maladies increased and multiplied so much, that deprived of all strength of body she was entirely confined to her bed, so that for the space of thirty-three years before her death she did not touch the ground. And her nourishment after the first three years until the nineteenth year of her sickness was of a food slight and little, and that cannot be conceived sufficient for the sustenance of so very ailing a human life. Sometimes she took a small piece of apple warmed over the fire, sometimes a little bread with a slight sip of white beer, sometimes a little fresh milk. Afterwards, however, she could not take such things for weakness of body; for some years she drank through the week half a pint of pure wine, without any admixture, which nevertheless later for some years it was necessary to mingle with water. Sometimes also she would eat a little spice of sugar or cinnamon, or musk, or grapes. But when she could no longer take these eating or sucking, she took only water, namely half a pint of the water of the Meuse a week; which by a special gift of God brought her such sweetness, that it surpassed all flavour of wine; for the which she used to give great thanks to God. At the same time she received this favour from God, that by taste alone she distinguished between the water of the Meuse when the tide was in and when the tide was out, when she took the cup brought her, with a draught therefrom.[1] For many years there was that also which is more to be wondered at, that she had no sleep and took no bodily food or drink except the body of Christ, the sole remedy of all her pains, and a most sweet solace, most savoury to her above all food.[2]

[1] Schiedam is at a sufficient distance from the sea to have the Meuse water there usually fresh; but at full moon it would be salty enough when the tide was in to make a noticeable difference to the poor sufferer who took no other drink

[2] This abstinence from all food was made the subject of a rigorous inquiry by the town authorities. See *Introduction*. For the rest, as Huysmans remarks, no inquiry could be more critical than that which would be provoked in such a case by the curiosity or envy of neighbours.

CHAPTER VII

OF THE VARIOUS ILLNESSES AND PAINS THAT TORMENTED HER DAY AND NIGHT

In this virgin was accomplished what is read of blessed Job. "In the night my bone is pierced with sorrows; and they that feed upon me do not sleep: with the multitude of them my garment is consumed" (Job xxx 17). And so with the failure of medical arts and of the nourishment of food, her weakness daily grew worse. And the maiden pitiably afflicted lay upon a hard couch and was eaten by worms which, rising from her virginal body out of the putrefaction, consumed her flesh: and nevertheless no stench proceeded from them. These worms were of a grey colour full of grey water, having black heads, large as the thickness of the end of a spindle, long as the measure of the small joint of a man's finger.

She had also, disciple of the holy Trinity, in her body three large openings, from one of which in the stomach the aforesaid worms sometimes flowed

ST. LYDWINE *of* SCHIEDAM

abundantly. To this wound was placed a plaster made up of fresh wheat and honey, that the generated worms might feed on this mixture and other ingredients; for else they would have eaten her even to death. And when these plasters were taken off to be changed, there remained on them little grey worms with black heads, giving forth from them no bad odour, but offering a sweet smell to those who beheld them. The same virgin then was corrupt in the lower part of the body with a permanent and large wound; and that her holy bowels might not altogether fall out, they closed the opening with some soft bandage.

It happened at that time that the famous physician of the Duke of Holland, Master Godfrey of Hague, came to visit this maiden with the Duchess Margaret, to examine the cause of her maladies; in order to give the maiden some wholesome remedy if he could. Who, as was permissible and befitting, having seen some of the intestines of her stomach which were taken from her body and placed in a dish, found that the aforesaid worms came from the putrefaction of the spinal cord of her back; and that that putrefaction was caused by a natural consequence, because she ate no salt. After which, seeing that he could do no good for her, he bade that the intestines be replaced again in her stomach. The same doctor also remarked, that in a short time she would be dropsical. And she contracted this dropsy about nineteen years before her death, during which she took neither food nor drink nor sleep. And as she received no nourishment, so she voided no natural superfluities.

About the year of the Lord, 1412, this sacred plant of God, dug about by the long hoe of suffering, from the vehemence of her pains vomited by little pieces her lung and liver, with several intestines, but without any stench, as was proved by many. For those who touched them with their hands, felt a sweetness cling to their hands for nearly a day. From the fourteenth year until the twenty-first she could nowise move or turn herself; and she lay on her back that seven years and after even to death, nor could any part of her body move, except her head and left arm with the shoulder. But when she was moved or turned in bed, then it was necessary to bind round her shoulders with a cloth or soft bandage; otherwise there was a danger that she would fall to pieces.

Very many other maladies also the virgin of Christ girded with most cruel scourges suffered; which were inflicted upon her not to the loss of her soul, but to her greater merit as on holy Job, so that afterwards she might be the more capable and meet for angelic and heavenly consolations, the more distressed and desolate she lay upon earth. She often had excessive headaches even unto death, very often manifold toothache even unto death, divers fevers also even unto death, a long dropsy even unto death, at the time of pestilence three abscesses, a very great stone also before death, with which likewise she paid the debt of death. All this for very many years she suffered most patiently, that her soul might be saved for ever, and with Christ exult in the delights of Paradise. For the more bodily sicknesses abounded in her, so much the greater grew in her the love, strong as death, of God and her neighbour. For from the plenitude of her charity and the urgency of her internal fervour, she dared in a certain way to provoke the

Lord to multiply upon her miseries and pains. And the Lord hearkening to her prayers, when she had two abscesses in her body, added a third on her breast. In fine, she suffered from all the common infirmities wherewith men are usually afflicted, the which she lovingly bore with wondrous and unparalleled patience for the love of Christ, mindful of all His even greater dolours. There was scarcely any part of her body which did not waste away with some special affliction of suffering. For on her forehead she had a fracture extending to the middle of the nose; likewise on the lower lip and chin a cleft congealed with blood, and because of this malady she could hardly speak. Her right eye was altogether sightless; and her left remained so weak, that it could make use of no material light by day or by night, yea even she felt torture from any brightness of light. Wherefore she constantly lay in darkness; and a simple curtain surrounded and veiled the place of her bed, so that seldom was she openly seen by men. But yet she very often saw an angel of light to the comfort of her exceeding great torture.

CHAPTER VIII

OF THE SEVERITY OF HER FEVER AND A FRESH DISEASE IN HER LEG

This rose of Christ suffered long and divers fevers, often quartan, often tertian, and often daily. Amid which thorns of affliction she simply gave up her body to the will and chastisement of God to be crucified; at Whose bidding all things were ordered unto the good of her soul, and much better than any man could foreknow or design. And in fact the tertian fevers she endured for seventeen years and more: which for the salvation and redemption of souls, she was willingly ready to bear even to death. The attacks of these fevers was as follows. For first she felt an indescribable heat, which was followed by an indescribable cold. Then again the aforesaid heat and afterwards the intense cold returned: which vicissitudes lasted for nearly half the year. But afterwards she would have the same fever the other way; for first she was in a great and indescribable cold, and then in an immense heat, which lasted until the torture finally

ST. LYDWINE *of* SCHIEDAM

ceased. But when the fever gave over she would be so insensible that, unconscious of herself, she could neither hear nor speak. For when she felt the attack of the fever she applied herself to exercise of the Lord's Passion, commending herself and her sufferings to the Passion of Him in Whom all bitter things are sweetened. Who often withdrew her by excess of mind from corporal things so that she noticed neither herself nor anything else whatsoever. And during this fever, she sent out a certain red water from her mouth; and when she was questioned whence such matter came, seeing that she took neither food nor drink, she answered by a question thus. "Tell me whence so much sap comes in the vine; which during winter seems withered and almost dead?" But the virgin of Christ was comforted exceedingly in her so weak body by taking up a good meditation on God; and she was much more refreshed thereby than another would have been by most costly foods. And if the presence of men and her maladies had not hindered her, she would not have wondered if on account of the abundance of divine grace each month, she had fattened the flesh in her body beyond the measure of a Hamburg vat.

Once also before the beginning of the fast, while the people were amusing themselves in the square near her cell, she grieved much over these vanities, and prayed God that if it were pleasing to Him in her regard, or if He Himself wrought those things in her which she suffered, He would deign to show her this by the sign of a new illness. And the Lord, hearing her prayers, gave her in one of her legs a fresh troublesome disease. With which malady indeed she was so grievously afflicted until the next Easter, that conscious of her weakness she did not dare to beg for a further increase of her infirmities. But she was wont to say in her daily sicknesses to some who constantly assisted her, that she was quite willing to bear them for forty years; yea even to the end of the world for the conversion of any sinner, or for the deliverance of any faithful soul from the pains of Purgatory. For although she was weighed down by such great maladies, she retained the full use of her senses, and a quick intelligence and memory, so that to many who came from distant parts to visit her asking advice, she afforded comfort in spiritual things as well as healing in bodily needs. Many women also labouring in childbirth, she relieved by loving compassion and the assistance of her counsel. In the midst of these divine gifts she was not puffed up, nor did she presume loftily concerning her future glory, but bowing down her heart in humility, she most patiently bore all her burdens in charity, and feared as if she were to suffer Purgatory after this life. But she merited such grace with God that the holy angels numbered the steps of those who visited her for the sake of devotion. Wherefore she used to console her visitors, who sometimes complained of the weariness of their journey; that they should not grieve for their fatigue, because God would render them a good reward for their toil.

CHAPTER IX

OF THE HARDNESS OF HER BED AND THE COLD SHE SUFFERED IN WINTER

Our Lord and Saviour Jesus Christ commending St. John Baptist amid many virtues for his rough raiment and abstinence, added also this. "For they, that are clothed in soft garments, are in the houses of kings" (Matt. xi 8). But this virgin was not nourished in a royal palace; but in her father's house, oppressed by divers and grievous maladies, she used for a time under the stress of her exceeding great weakness a small feather bed, not to caress the flesh by softness, but to support the weakness of nature a little in order that it might serve the spirit. But when from the multitude of her wounds she could not bear a bed of feathers, because the feathers hardened by the oozing matter tormented her as she lay, the easy bed was taken away and for a time she lay upon the bare straw; for three years she even rested uneasily with her naked back upon a hard plank taken from the bottom of a bin. Lying therefore upon wretched straw, the poor virgin full of sores, the sister of the beggar and poor man Lazarus, left her bed to the son and daughter of her brother for their rest; who day and night by mutual charity in turn ministered to her needs.

About the year of the Lord, 1408, so

severe a cold reigned through the world the whole winter, that in duration and bitterness it afflicted men much more than usual, and destroyed the plants of the earth and the fishes under the water. In this most terrible winter the sick slave of Christ covered with wounds was frequently so frozen from the fearful cold and her nakedness, that her limbs became black, and the tears of her eyes congealed; so that she was unable to see except by melting them with the application of heat. Very many other pains also she suffered at that time from the presence of the cold, such as could scarcely be endured by the strong, and if the Author of nature had not supernaturally cared for and preserved her, she would undoubtedly have lost her life. In the accumulation of all these so many miseries and needs of her own, as a kind mother and loving nurse she was ever mindful of other poor, taking away from her own necessaries in order to aid them in their want. However, the rich of this world who live in luxury, and exult in much wealth to the loss of their souls, were entirely forgetful of her, and stretched not a helping hand to the poor sufferer. Many also not knowing her holiness despised her, and deeming her mad mocked at her mental ecstasies. Then was fulfilled in her, that which is read of holy Job. "The simplicity of the just man is laughed to scorn; and the lamp despised in the thoughts of the rich" (Job xii 4, 5).

CHAPTER X

OF HER WATCHINGS AND STRUGGLE AGAINST SLEEP

It seems very wonderful and almost incredible to many, how the weak flesh could last in so many sufferings and pains, which for so long a time was nourished by neither food nor drink nor sleep. But if we remember the divine power, which makes possible the impossible, [we can understand that] the maid was able to bear all things in Him Who strengthened her; for that which is beyond nature was brought to pass by the work of God. Witnesses are the many martyrs and virgins thrown into the flames, who by God's ordering and protection were found not only very patient in their torments, but even full of joy; and what is more, they remained unharmed amid blows, swords, and fires. The hand of God then is not shortened, nor the arm of the Almighty feeble to save them that hope in Him; but in every place and time the Lord is near them that call upon and love Him in truth. In this feeble servant of God therefore let the work of the Divinity be acknowledged, and the weakness of man cease to distrust. Which, while it depends upon its own opinions for natural reasons, very often fails and is blinded in its search. For nature must needs be silent when the divine speaks; and earthly things yield when the things of Heaven are treated. This virgin, then, lying so long on the bed of pain, was not forgetful of her Creator, but mindful of the name of the Lord day and night, she gave herself fervently to holy meditations and prayers; and especially at the time of the Divine Office and the celebration of the High Mass. Whence how strongly she struggled against and overcame sleepiness, is worth the telling and pleasant to hear. It is commonly the habit of many men, to be more tempted to sleep at the time of the Divine Office, whether from their own weakness or from the suggestion of the devil, who ever strives to oppose man's salvation and devout prayers. When therefore the scholar of Christ, having learnt to pray often, felt herself more than usually weighed down and tempted by the spirit of torpor and drowsiness at the time of the Divine Office, although she was wont to sleep very little at that period, nevertheless she grieved much within herself over this temptation of sloth, and dared not yield to it. Her confessor therefore fearing that danger threatened her if she did not sleep, urged her with a view to her health not to resist drowsiness any more, but whatever feast might come at whatever time or hour to set herself to sleep. On a certain Easter Sunday, then, when the same temptation coming grievously molested her; she mindful of the Lord very strongly resisted the drowsiness, according to what is written. "Resist the devil and he will fly from you." Having then gained this one victory over sleep, she was so strengthened against it by God, that she never slept after that until her death, nor was ever tempted with drowsiness. For as the holy angels, resisting the first temptation of pride, were confirmed in grace, and those who consented were cast out of Heaven, so to this victorious virgin was given the gift of inviolable fortitude in many watchings and in stripes afflicting her beyond measure; by which she was proved as gold is tried in a burning furnace (Wisdom iii 6).

CHAPTER XI

OF THE POVERTY AND ENDURANCE OF HER FATHER

This holy virgin's father, Peter Johns above named, although he had come to such poverty, that he toilsomely obtained the necessaries of life by keeping the night watches in the city, nevertheless he was so honest and conscientious that in his need he was unwilling to spend the alms of his daughter, saying that they would be the sins of men. Therefore he wished and he persuaded his beloved child, that she would use herself what was offered for God's sake, and expend it on pious purposes. It happened then in the aforesaid severe winter, that his limbs were numbed in the night watches from the excessive cold, and the big toe of the right foot was frostbitten. In which case indeed the probity of the man is shown; since he chose rather to endure the rigour of the cold, and to support himself by the labour of watching, than to eat up the alms of the poor. For it is written. "Thou shalt eat the labour of thy hands: blessed art thou and it shall be well with thee."

At the same time Duke William, with the Duchess Lady Margaret and a large company, entered the city of Schiedam; and noticing the poverty of Peter, a most noble man of a military family, moved with a pious compassion, out of reverence for the holiness of his daughter, he bade him ask with confidence from him, as much as he thought would suffice for his yearly expenses and needs. Who replying simply, asked for twelve crowns of France. The Duke himself marvelled at the modesty of the petitioner, and ordered that these crowns should be given him every year; declaring that he was ready to give double the amount, that he might not longer suffer such want. And this money was at first indeed faithfully paid; but afterwards it was bestowed on him less willingly, for the favour of man is quickly exhausted in giving: blessed therefore the man who has his treasure in Heaven. And receiving this alms from the aforesaid Duke William, Peter, not elated because of the benefit bestowed on him, but grateful to God, constantly visited the church, intent on devout prayer as best he could, perfectly contented with his daily food and a moderate raiment.

CHAPTER XII

OF THE ILLUSION OF SATAN WHO CAST HER FATHER INTO A DITCH

And when this devout Peter was so weak from old age, that he could scarcely walk without falling frequently from any slight cause and returning home injured, nevertheless he did not refrain from visiting the church on account of his bruises and falls, but as if still possessed of youth, drawn by fervent devotion visited the temple of God, even against the wish of his daughter. For the holy child was anxious for her father's safety, more grieving and fearing for his danger than for the scourge of her own disease.

On one occasion, going out on the vigil of Pentecost to hear Vespers, he met the devil, who appeared to him in the likeness of one he knew, as it seemed outwardly. Who, wishing to deceive the simple man, suggested that they should go for a stroll outside the city, alleging that they would return in good time for the hour of Vespers. And he, not knowing that it was Satan, agreed, and they went together beyond the city gate to the place called Damlaen. Then the devil showing the wickedness of his deceit, suddenly rushed upon Peter, and before he saw or knew, cast him into a ditch and disappeared. And as he was there beginning to drown and there was no one at hand to aid, by divine providence a certain carter, an acquaintance of his, contrary to his wont came by the same way from the country with his waggon, wishing to enter the city, and he saw Peter lying in the ditch, and quite unable to help himself. And being moved with compassion he at once drew him out of the mud; and setting the injured man upon his cart, brought him back safe to the town. And immediately a false report unexpectedly assailed the ears of all; as if Peter had been drowned and was dead. And this news so afflicted the ears of his daughter, that she could never afterwards recall that vigil without deep anguish because of the suffering of her father. For the crafty enemy reckoned to cause a great catastrophe to the virgin, if he added her father's distress to the pain of her own wounds. But God, the helper in afflictions and the comforter of the sorrowful, in a short while turned the father's weariness into rest, his grief into joy, his poverty into heavenly riches. For, consoled by the blessed virgin, he was snatched by a speedy and blissful end from the troubles of this world and the guiles of the devil.

CHAPTER XIII

OF THE DEATH OF HER FATHER ON THE VIGIL OF THE CONCEPTION OF THE BLESSED VIRGIN MARY

A few days before the Conception of the Blessed Virgin Mary, the devout maiden Lydwine, the daughter of Peter, foreknew that her father was about to pass from this world. For she said that she had heard in secret from her father, that the Blessed Virgin Mary had entered into a pact with him, and had promised that she would call him from the present world about this festival. Which also came to pass as she foretold. The most faithful maiden therefore warned Master John the priest who had come to her for advice; that the same day he should go to Ouderschie to celebrate, so that on the morrow nothing might be wanting for her father's funeral. After these words the death of her father took place on the vigil of the Conception of the Blessed Virgin, according to the vision and prophecy revealed before.

And after his death, although the maiden, deprived of the temporal solace of her father's presence, had asked and had been assured of the salvation of her father, the perverse demons, the enemies of all the good, sometimes saddened her exceedingly, asserting that they had her father with them in the state of damnation. Whereupon she commenced to weep inconsolably, as if what she had heard from the demons were true. Whence also when questioned by the members of the household why she wept so much, she answered, "I know that all is very well with my father, and nevertheless the demons say that he is lost." On one occasion, therefore, when she was being conducted by a holy angel to the gardens of paradise, the demons besetting her path, showed her a devil transformed into the likeness of her father, mocking and tormenting, saying, "Ah, ah, look here, we have thy father." Then she, knowing that the act of the devil was a vain illusion and not the truth, said that this could not be her father. And at once they vanished as smoke; and the maiden joyously continued her journey with the angel guide.

CHAPTER XIV

OF THE DEATH OF JOHN PETERS HER GRANDFATHER AND HIS LONG CONTINENCE

We must not pass over in silence the righteousness and continence of John

Peters, who was the grandsire of this virgin and the parent of her father, to the praise of God and to exalt the dignity of this good family. This John Peters, then, of praiseworthy repute and life, after the death of his wife remained a widower more than fifty years, until he attained the ripe old age of nearly ninety. And he practised such continence and abstinence, that as a solitary turtledove and lover of chastity, after the death of his wife he never knew woman. Moreover, for the preservation of this continent life he fasted twice a week on bread and water, and once only, to wit on Sunday, he took meat at dinner. And at his death Satan the malignant ensnarer, seeing that he could not approach him, set up such a tumult in other parts of the house, that the earthenware vessels were broken, but without any loss or spilling of the butter which was kept in one of these jars. Nor is it strange if the devil dared beset and harm the most faithful servant of Christ, who inflicted the annoyance of temptations on Christ in His fast; from whom nevertheless he departed vanquished and put to shame, for the fraudulent one was unable to deceive the Almighty. And as the holy angels after the departure of the temptation drew near to Christ, so it is to be piously believed that the soul of John Peters was guarded by angels, and after the death of the flesh blissfully conducted to Christ whom he served in life.

CHAPTER XV

OF THE DEATH OF PETRONILLA HER MOTHER

It seems fitting also to insert in the present page the passing away of the noble woman Petronilla, the mother of this holy virgin, and to associate the woman to these noble men in due order of virtue. After eight years then had passed from the commencement of the virgin Lydwine's illness, her mother Petronilla, who had been most attentive to her ailing daughter, also fell into a sickness of the body; of which, as of one of the children of Eve, she died. When therefore she was nearing death, and giving heed to her imperfection, mourned that she had not lived righteously enough, she begged of her beloved child whom she knew to be pleasing and dear to God, that she would aid her when departed by her merits and prayers. And she, casting all her thought and hope upon the Lord, said that she was quite willing to die, renouncing her own choice so much, that she would not that the smallest little worm should die in her stead. Hearing this, the holy and faithful daughter, deeply touched, and compassionating her mother from her heart, urged her with holy words to trust in the goodness of God; so as to bear with patience the scourge of the Lord and death which none can escape. And therefore for her succour she most willingly offered her, and utterly resigned whatever meritorious good she had hitherto gained in the exercise of virtue, in toils and the endurance of patience. When her mother had heard and gratefully accepted this, trusting in the mercy of God she commended herself into the hands of her Creator. And the virgin, abiding faithful to her mother through all unto death, and considering what she had now done, and deeming herself as emptied of all her former good works, to commence afresh a new penance, girded herself with a hair girdle, hard and broad, adding new pain to the old, that God might be propitious to her and to every faithful soul. But after some years the virgin girded with the hair cloth, when on account of the dropsical humours of her body, the first girdle was rotted, again with mighty zeal girds herself with another new one, and successively with many others that were laid aside as worn out, until with the last she passed from this life.

CHAPTER XVI

OF HER STATE AFTER HER MOTHER'S DEATH, AND HER PITY FOR THE POOR

After the death of her mother, the virgin, mindful of her mother's love, to pay the debt of filial affection, did not bury the talent entrusted to her in the earth; but the few silver ornaments, and all the other household utensils left by her mother for her use because of her pressing need, she sold at a low price; and the sum gained thereby, she so generously distributed to the poor, that in consoling the wretched she was brought to the utmost poverty. Those things also which she received from the faithful in alms, she passed on so cheerfully to the poor, as if she seemed to have no thought at all of temporal things. Thence from the money she had and from what was given for her needs, she sent to divers poor persons bread, meat, dried fish, and cheeses, and a measure of beer with a jug which her loving mother had left her; and if God bestowed anything further upon her, she faithfully gave it away. And while she sent these things by her attendants, in the meantime she gave herself to the leisure of devout prayers, rendering thanks to the giver of all good things, who had granted her something for the use of the poor.

CHAPTER XVII

OF THE BURNING OF HER BED WHICH SHE PUT OUT WITH ONE HAND WITHOUT ANY INJURY

On one occasion the brother of this virgin, who after his father also kept the night watches, set a lighted candle near the head of her bed in a high place of the corner and went out. And this falling on the straw burnt a great portion of the bed, but she with her face covered was engaged in her usual devotion. At length coming to herself and opening her eyes, she saw herself lying in the midst of a fire and no one near to put it out; by the help of God with her left hand she extinguished all the flame without any injury to her hand, to the great wonder of all who, coming in the morning to her, saw what had happened in the burning of the bed while the virgin remained unharmed. Nevertheless she at that time did not use a bed, but the children of her brother did, who were devoted in serving her; for she herself in her illness lay upon straw.

CHAPTER XVIII

OF THE ASHES MINISTERED TO HER BY AN ANGEL AT THE BEGINNING OF LENT

The most devout maiden, after the manner of other Christians, was wont on the Wednesday of the beginning of Lent to receive with humble reverence from the hand of her confessor blessed ashes which he, taking from the church, brought with him to sign her. One Lent, therefore, on Ash Wednesday, her confessor coming in to her, asked her whether she wished him to bring ashes with him from the church. The virgin answered saying, "It may be good that you do so. However God has provided me with ashes." For the angel of the Lord had been with her a little before, and had signed her forehead with ashes. But that her confessor might be assured of this; taking his hand she placed it upon the ashes so that he might touch them, and he found that beyond doubt it was so. Moreover, that he might share in so great a favour, with her permission he brought his forehead in touch with hers. The angel of the Lord also taught her that those who receive the holy ashes should receive them with a light and a cross—to wit, a burning candle with the cross on the penny brought to the altar—as a sign that they offered themselves with the light of faith by true subjection and mortification to God.[1]

[1] The Bollandists remark that they can find no trace of the custom here mentioned.

CHAPTER XIX

OF THE WINE MIRACULOUSLY PLACED IN HER CUP

A certain poor woman afflicted with the falling sickness was begging a drink from door to door. And when from horror of her infirmity all avoided her and shut their doors, the virgin, compassionate and shunning no one in misery, learning of her sad case, gave word that the beggar, who was near her house, should be called to her and brought in. Coming in then to the virgin, she begged the alms of a drink. Then the sick virgin, pitying the poor beggar, since she had nothing better at hand to give her, bade her take the cup of wine standing on a shelf and drink it. "Take that cup, child," she said, "and drink what wine is in it." And when, having emptied this, the thirsty woman asked for still more, the virgin answered that she knew not what other drink there would be in the house. But that she might not go away sad and unsatisfied, she gave her a penny to buy a drink therewith at a tavern. After this, as evening drew on, the virgin's lips became parched with thirst. She therefore asked her father, who was living at that time, to hand her a little wine to refresh the dryness of her thirst. He answered, "Certainly," and taking the aforesaid cup to fulfil his daughter's request, at once he spilled over himself the wine which by God's will had been placed therein. And so for the little which she had graciously given to the poor woman in her need, she received from God wine of a much better sort and in greater quantity. And when the father told his daughter this, she in wonder gave thanks to God from her heart. And this wine was red and so well tempered, that it was not necessary to mingle water with it, as she was wont to do with the other. And this wine lasted from the feast of St. Remigius[1] until the feast of the Conception of the Blessed Virgin Mary.[2] At which time she received a visit from a certain good matron named Catherine Simons, who was accustomed from a special devotion to supply her with wine. She, not knowing the mystery of

[1] October 1st.   [2] December 8th.

the wine given by God, wishing to provide some better and fresh, as thinking this wine spoilt from being there too long, poured it all out, and thus she no longer enjoyed that heavenly favour. Nevertheless the virgin told her friend, the aforenamed Catherine, before she poured out the wine, that this wine was quite suitable and sufficient for her, and that she had never tasted the like before. This sign of grace was wrought for her in the year of the Lord one thousand and four hundred and twelve, while she still drank half a pint of wine a week.

CHAPTER XX

OF THE MONEY PAID FOR HER BROTHER AND MULTIPLIED IN HER PURSE

After this, in the year of the Lord 1423, the brother of this virgin, William Peters, died, and he left after him certain debts which his children could not pay. When the most compassionate virgin learnt this, having sold the jewelry left her by her mother's legacy, she amassed a sum of eight Holland pounds, which she had changed into pieces of one coin which she knew better, and placed in a purse by her side. One day, therefore, towards evening she called Nicholas her kinsman who was dwelling with her, and sent by his hand to pay her brother's debts to all his creditors, where she knew that they lived. Having therefore paid all the debts which she knew were due, she told Nicholas to look into the purse, if anything had remained in it. Who answered, that most certainly much money was left in it. At once she bade him count the same. And when he had counted, he said that he found the first eight pounds, and that there was something over. Then she forbade him count more, and giving thanks to God for His wonderful gift, she declared that that purse should henceforth be called the purse of Jesus, and that from it what was needful should be given to the poor. From this therefore she distributed freely to the needy, when she had not other money. But if sometimes she had some money either her own or received in alms, she would first give this, but when she had not any other, she gave so generously from this purse of Jesus, that little remained in it. But the mercy of God Almighty provided, that always for the use of the poor all sufficiency abounded therein, as at the word of Elias the cruse of oil failed not in the widow's house. Sometimes also she handed this money to one of her special friends to be counted, and when he had counted it a second or a third time, he always found that it had increased by three, or four, or five pieces. Having therefore paid her brother's debts from this purse, she distributed more than forty pounds from the same, as she revealed to some of her very familiar friends. And by this miracle God made evidently known, that [even] an accountant might have strong faith in the gifts of God which were wrought in her.

CHAPTER XXI

OF THE HAM GIVEN TO THE POOR, AND MIRACULOUSLY REPLACED BY ANOTHER

When on one occasion the pious and pitiful virgin Lydwine had learnt that some poor people had not eaten meat for a long time because of their want, and as she had not at that moment any flesh meat to give them, she sent to the house of a certain friend, begging him to boil a ham and send it to her. Which he willingly did, and sent. And she divided the meat cooked and prepared into parts, and without delay sent it on to the aforesaid poor whom she knew to be in need. But the almighty and merciful God, Who knows the hearts of all and leaves no good unrewarded, rendered a swift return to the charity of this benefactor even in the present. For entering his house, and looking up by chance to the pieces of meat that were hanging, he saw, which is wonderful to relate, in the place of the ham taken away and sent to the virgin for the refreshment of the poor, another hanging better and finer. Which many hearing, rendered thanks to Almighty God; and thereafter were much more devoted to her, willingly giving whatever white meats the virgin asked of them to feed the poor.

CHAPTER XXII

OF THE MEAT AND PEAS GIVEN TO THE POOR, AND MULTIPLIED

It likewise happened once in autumn that the virgin had a quarter of a heifer, which she had bought, salted in the fourth part of a barrel, and also half a certain measure of peas she procured for the need of the poor, wishing with these to succour during the winter some poor people who lived at home. When therefore she had sent of the aforesaid meat to nearly thirty-six poor families, her messenger returning to her, said that he had distributed as much as he had first salted in the vessel, and that it was still diminished but little. In a like manner he had done with the peas; which also seemed to be very little lessened. Hearing which, the virgin considering the great goodness of God, and giving thanks to her heavenly Provider, said to the messenger: "O how great is the power of our Lord God, O how willingly we ought to give alms to the poor!" And of the aforesaid meat and peas ate also all who were in her house. So much had God blessed the above food, that when Easter was over about a half thereof remained. And all the winter she bade them prepare and cook a great pot of peas once or twice a week, and to give thereof to the poor with the aforesaid meat; imitating the example of Eliseus the prophet, who gave word that a pottage should be made ready for the sons of the prophets in a pot. And seldom did she send aught of this to anyone, but she added a coin small or great; if however she could have one. But neither did she give bread, without adding above some dish to be taken with the bread, or money to buy some condiment for the food. And not only the poor, but the rich also when they besought, she succoured from charity with her alms. It would be too long to recite each instance of what with unstinted hand, as she was able to possess, she gave to the sick, the weak, to men, and to women in childbirth.

CHAPTER XXIII

OF THE VISION OF A HEAVENLY TABLE FILLED BY THE ALMS OF THE POOR

And how pleasing to God were the alms of this virgin was revealed to her in ecstasy by a certain heavenly vision. Whence when she was rapt into Paradise she often saw first tables set, and covered with cloths of green silk, then her alms as if set by the citizens of heaven placed upon the same, never however lessened at all, but rather increased. But the liquor which she was wont to give in stone jars, she saw there presented in transparent vases as it were of crystal, and the dried fish given for her departed niece Petronilla likewise set. She saw also a glorious gathering of the blessed, all in their rank in different grades, approach the table in due time as if to take refreshment; and the priests holding aloft chalices, and the rest according to their dignity bearing befitting escutcheons, and herself also sometimes assist, and serve, or sit down with the guests; and drink given to them that were seated and to herself, and all filled with unspeakable joy and gladness, over such great charity shown them by her. If ever on those tables she saw nothing of her own almsgiving represented, she was greatly ashamed, as if all had brought their respective portions, but she herself had contributed nothing. Whence both for the sake of increasing the glory of almsgiving, and because of the confusion suffered, she made haste afterwards to add to her alms. Sometimes, however, the angel her guide led her to a certain cell apart and spacious, in which he served her her refreshment. This refection, even if she felt it to be ineffable, nevertheless as much as she was able to describe it, she said was a certain heavenly and divine light, whereby she was divinely refreshed and inebriated. Sometimes also by prayers she obtained of the angel that she might take one of those who were familiar and dear to her to taste these things; and although seeing in their sleep, they felt that something of the kind was happening to them, nevertheless it was in a very different and inferior manner than befell herself.

Here endeth the First Part of the Book.

Life of Lydwine, Virgin
Part II

PART II

PROLOGUE TO THE SECOND PART OF THE LIFE OF THE SAME VIRGIN

Having spoken briefly of the many diseases and sufferings of this virgin, and also of the gracious works of her mercy and of certain miraculous deeds to the praise of God Almighty; now also in due course of her spiritual gifts and divine consolations and frequent raptures, somewhat must be said and humbly related to the edification of the religious.

THE CHAPTERS OF THE SECOND PART OF THE SAME

Chap.   Page

I. Of the beginning of her spiritual consolations through the recollection of the Lord's Passion . . 109

II. Of her rapture into the Holy Land, and to the sacred places of the city of Rome 113

III. Of the wonderful brightness and sweetness appearing in her cell . 116

IV. Of the vision on Christmas night, and the abundance of milk in her breasts . . 118

V. Of the cypress rod which an angel brought her from Paradise . 121

VI. Of the bereavement of the angelic brightness on account of the presence of another hiding in her cell . . 125

VII. Of her rapture to the regions of Purgatory, and to the joys of Paradise, whence she brought back a veil given her by the Blessed Virgin 128

CONTENTS

Chap.		Page
VIII.	Of the glorious crown prepared for her because of the insults and wounds inflicted on her by the men of Picardy	133
IX.	Of the patience and death of Petronilla, this virgin's niece	140
X.	Of the withdrawal of divine consolation, which the virgin suffered on account of her grief for her dead niece	143
XI.	Of the devout youth Gerard who had become a hermit, and of the pilgrims who visited him	147
XII.	Of the happy end of Master Wermbold, priest, this virgin's faithful friend	153
XIII.	Of her divers raptures and her knowledge of the state of certain religious	157
XIV.	Of the appearance and knowledge of the angelic brightness about her	161
XV.	Of the wonderful manner of her interior pain before the rapture of her spirit	163
XVI.	Of her spirit of prophecy, whereby she revealed to others many hidden things	165
XVII.	Of a certain departed sacristan and many other dead	167
XVIII.	Of her caution and prudence concerning the revelation of the state of the departed	170
XIX.	Of the temptation of a certain man delivered by the advice of the virgin from the snare of the devil	172

CONTENTS

Chap.		Page
XX.	Of a woman freed by the merits of the blessed Virgin Mary from the gulf of despair	174
XXI.	Of her grace of great compunction and abundant shedding of tears in the Communion of the body of Christ	176
XXII.	Of her insatiable desire to communicate often, and of the appearance of a child crucified	179
XXIII.	Of the fever of the child Baldwine, and of Master John her confessor	185
XXIV.	Of her suffering from stone, and her foreknowledge before the day of her death	187
XXV.	Of the grace on Easter night and the prophecy of her death	190
XXVI.	Of her happy death and sufferings at the last	192
XXVII.	Of the wonderful placing of her arms, and the shrouding of her body	195
XXVIII.	Of the wonderful beauty and aspect of her countenance	199
XXIX.	Of the flocking of visitors to her dead body	201
XXX.	Of the stains which she contracted from the touch of unclean men	202
XXXI.	Of her reverential burial	203
XXXII.	Of the miracles after her death	206
XXXIII.	The narration of three miracles	206

CHAPTER I

OF THE BEGINNING OF HER SPIRITUAL CONSOLATIONS THROUGH THE RECOLLECTION OF THE LORD'S PASSION

As of old through the mouth of the holy prophets God spoke His secrets to the comfort of His elect, so now also He speaks to them by the writings of the learned, and the examples of the good, lest perchance troubled by the divers tribulations of the world, or torn by scourges, they fall away from the hope and expectation of the joys to come. For holy David, to whom God revealed the hidden things of His wisdom (Ps. 18), says that he frequently received the consolations of God amid many adversities. "According to the multitude of my sorrows in my heart," he saith: "Thy consolations have given joy to my soul" (Ps. xciii 19). This sentence of Scripture God truly and manifestly fulfilled to the letter in this holy virgin, whom first He cleansed, inebriating by divers pains and bitternesses; but afterwards, amidst the bruises of many wounds visiting her, He poured in manifold consolations and rejoiced her. To repeat therefore something of what has been already said, after the first three or about four years from the beginning of her malady the virgin Lydwine was still impatient of the divine discipline, and not yet freely submissive to God, by Whom however nothing is done upon earth without cause; and when she saw her companions visiting her healthy and glad, and herself grievously sick, she desired rather health of body with the rest, than blessedness of soul through the virtue of patience. And because she did not yet savour spiritual things, and knew not what was more acceptable to God, therefore sometimes she complained, and grieved much over her pains, and wept so very bitterly, that she would accept comfort from no one. Going in to her, therefore, Master John Pot her confessor, who was wont to communicate her twice a year, strove to induce her by his words of consolation to moderate somewhat these tears and set a measure to her grief. Whence he persuaded her by a gentle exhortation to give and conform herself to the divine will, and to exercise herself in meditating upon the Lord's Passion, promising that by the means and aid thereof she would easily receive good consolation. Asking therefore the manner of this holy exercise, and having received from the priest the method of wholesome meditation, when she was desirous of exercising herself therein according to the formula given her, and did not immediately discover thence honey flowing from the rock, nor taste therein the bread of the prophet: overcome by weariness she soon cast aside as bitter absinthe that which she had received in her heart without fixedly rooting it therein. But when the same priest further insisted and urged her most strongly to do violence to herself and persevere in her beginnings, and overcome her distaste by a pious struggle, she, instructed by this excellent advice, easily yielded assent to the counsel of her priest. And at length the good habit of meditating upon God, gained by violence, brought her in due course of time such sweetness with the aid of heavenly grace, that denying herself perfectly she freely used to say, that if it were possible to recover the full health of her body by one *Hail Mary*, nevertheless she would not do it or desire it. Truly this was a change of the right hand of the Most High (Ps. lxxvi 11); Who opened His hand to the needy (Prov. xxxi 20), and comforted her in her long languishing by nights on the bed of her sorrow. For drawn and enticed by the hidden sweetness of the Lord's Passion, day and night at fixed intervals she used to turn over in thought the history of the same most sacred Passion divided into seven parts, according to the number of the Seven Canonical Hours; and finding therein a hidden manna, she was filled with the joy of such sweetness, that now not herself but Christ, Whose Passion she contemplated, seemed to endure what she had hitherto appeared to suffer in the body. Then taught of the Spirit by experience, she could fully say with Isaias, "Verily Thou art a hidden God" (Is. xlv 15). And again exclaim: "My soul hath desired Thee in the night;

yea, and with my spirit within me in the morning early I will watch to Thee" (Is. xxvi 9).

CHAPTER II

OF HER RAPTURE INTO THE HOLY LAND, AND TO THE SACRED PLACES OF THE CITY OF ROME

While then the sick virgin earnestly occupied herself every day in exercises of the Lord's Passion, sometimes she was rapt by a holy angel to the places of the Holy Land in which Our Saviour by His birth, life, and suffering wrought the mysteries of man's redemption. When therefore on Mount Calvary, where the Lord was crucified, or at the other holy places, she was admitted to kiss the Lord's cross or His wounds; and for the refreshment of her tribulations sucked honey out of the rock, and oil from the hardest stone, and attained to the embrace of the transfixed feet, and to the expiring of her Spouse crucified for love, then also after the example of Him Whom she sought and loved, she commended her spirit into His hands. And although she often passed from the wounds of the flesh to penetrate the abysmal openings of the divinity through the rapture of contemplation, so that for the abundance of spiritual graces and sweetness she ceased to feel the sufferings of the body, nevertheless she was sometimes afflicted by such great fresh maladies, that even returning from those sweet kisses of the Lord's cross and His wounds she brought back certain ulcers imprinted upon the lips of her mouth. Which indeed by the ordinance of God was wrought, so that not only according to the multitude of sorrows in her heart the divine consolations should rejoice her soul within, but that also, according to the multitude of the divine consolations, her tribulations and afflictions suddenly arising should sadden and humble her without; that thereby openly and frequently tried she might know by contrary vicissitudes what things she had received from God, and what she had of herself. Then finally the angel said to her: "These ulcers thou hast therefore received in thy body, that thou mayest know that thou art rapt also in the body."

Another time likewise, when she was passing through the aforesaid most happy regions, and for the slipperiness of the path could not keep her footing, she said that she felt in the body a certain fall on the right foot, and that she suffered pain from that fall and from the sprain of the same foot. For from that injury she contracted such a swelling and blackening and pain in her ankle, that even for several days she was tormented thereby.

In a like manner she was once rapt to the sacred places of the city of Rome. And while she was going between some of the chief churches, and was proceeding with outstretched arms between shrubs and thorn bushes, from the same bushes she received a thorn in her fingers and brought it back with her, from the pain of which, as from the other maladies, she suffered not a little for nearly two days. On account of these bodily injuries then which thus she brought back, she was wont to say, according to the word of the angel, that she thought she had been rapt in the body also. But how these bodily raptures took place, the angel himself knew who conducted her and bore witness thereof.

At times our Saviour Jesus Christ, surrounded by the heavenly hosts, entering her cell as a king with his princes, set Himself at table, and seated in order around her bed, they most fully refreshed her with heavenly meats. And what wonder if she needed not bodily food, who was now nourished with the angels on heavenly dishes, as the Saviour Himself answered the devil tempting Him over bread: "It is written, not in bread alone doth man live, but in every word that proceedeth from the mouth of God" (Matt. iv 4).

CHAPTER III

OF THE WONDERFUL BRIGHTNESS AND SWEETNESS APPEARING IN HER CELL

Apart from her mental illumination, over which great men of letters and religious, versed in spiritual studies, who often spoke with her, and not understanding it wondered exceedingly, very often by day and night when she was visited by the angel, or returned from the contemplation of the things above, she was discovered by her companions to be surrounded by so great a divine brightness, that, seeing the splendour, struck with exceeding fear, they dared not approach nigh to her. And although she always lay in darkness, and material light was unbearable to her eyes, nevertheless the divine light was very agreeable to her, whereby her cell was often so wondrously flooded by night, that to the beholders the cell itself appeared full of material lamps or fires. Nor is it strange if she overflowed even in the body with divine brightness, who, according to the expression of blessed Paul, beholding the glory of the Lord with open face, was daily transformed into the same image from brightness to brightness as by the spirit of the Lord (2 Cor. iii 18). And not only was she wont to be surrounded by divine brightness, but with a wondrous sweetness also both herself and her cell were found to be redolent, so that those who entered thought that divers aromatic simples had been brought in and scattered there. And this wonderful sweetness was perceived when she was visited or touched by the Saviour or by the angel, or when she returned from

Heaven or the regions of Paradise. Which most sweet odour indeed not only breathed upon the scent through the nostrils, but redounded also on the taste of those who perceived it; and as strong a taste was felt upon the tongue, and bit the palate, as if they had eaten pepper or cinnamon. Chiefly, however, from the hand a fragrance of wondrous sweetness went forth when she had been led thereby by the holy angel to the joys above and thence brought back.

CHAPTER IV

OF THE VISION ON CHRISTMAS NIGHT, AND THE ABUNDANCE OF MILK IN HER BREASTS

A certain widow of good repute, by name Catherine, for some time dwelt in the house of this virgin. To her once before the nativity of Christ, it was made known by a vision concerning this virgin that on the Christmas night then at hand the breasts of this virgin would be filled with milk, and that Catherine herself was to take the same milk. When therefore the aforesaid widow had recounted this to the virgin, she from humility strove in a certain way to deny her words. At once the widow reproached the virgin that she should dare deny what had been revealed to her by an angel. Then the virgin, constrained by the widow's words, bade her prepare herself to share in this grace. When therefore she had devoutly prepared herself thereunto, according to the virgin's warning, she was not defrauded of her desire promised her by Heaven. For lo! on the night itself of the most sacred birth of the Lord, the virgin Lydwine, rapt in spirit, saw an innumerable multitude of maidens, at the head of whom as queen and mistress stood and presided the most holy mother of God, the ever Virgin Mary, among whom also she saw herself admitted in the choir of virgins to celebrate with joy the birth of Christ. By these virgins stood also a multitude of holy angels, as most noble clients and comrades, offering devout service to their friends, the virgins resplendent in the virtue of chastity. When therefore the hour of the Lord's birth arrived wherein the child-bearing Virgin brought forth the Christ, the breasts of all those virgins, and likewise of this virgin, were seen to swell for abundance of milk, and to have as much milk as the Blessed Virgin received in her virginal breasts to suckle Our Saviour when she had brought forth Christ into the light of the world. Therefore, after the manner of the Blessed Virgin, the breasts of all the others seemed to be filled with milk, as a sign that all those virgins were fit and worthy to suckle the Lord. But there was, as the virgin herself testified, so unspeakable a glory there, such as eye hath not seen, nor ear heard, nor hath it entered the heart of man to conceive, so that all could not be expressed by the tongue or written by letters. Meanwhile the widow, mindful of the aforesaid promise, comes in to the virgin, who, drawing her paps with her hand, abounded with such a flow of milk that the widow was satiated with a triple application of her lips, and for many days she remained without any desire to eat. And if the virgin had not bidden her, she would willingly have foregone bodily food. After this also she received the same grace and vision through contemplation two or three other years in her sacred breasts; but because at the hour assigned no one was present to witness it, therefore no one tasted of the grace offered. Praised then be Christ born of a Virgin, Who, to strengthen the faith of believers by works, made manifest in our days certain stupendous miracles in this ailing maiden.

CHAPTER V

OF THE CYPRESS ROD WHICH AN ANGEL BROUGHT HER FROM PARADISE

This virgin in the time of her sickness had a certain light twig with which to open or close the curtain of her bed, wherewith also she was wont to knock in case of need and call one of the household. It happened, therefore, on the occasion of the burning of the city, that many things were piled up round her bed on account of the threatening danger;[1] and thus by the carrying out

[1] See Part II, Chap. XVI. John Brugman in his second *Life* gives fuller details, from which it appears that the townspeople, fearing that Lydwine's cottage would take fire, stripped off the roof and left only the bare walls standing. But then to protect the

and the bringing back of things this rod also was lost, but where it was the virgin knew not. Afterwards, however, on the night of St. Apollinaris, bishop and martyr,[1] when the virgin for the intensity of the heat could scarcely draw her breath, she sought the rod to open the curtain, and found it not. Distressed therefore, she grieved much hereat, for she could not help herself; and there was no one else at hand to aid her. At once then the angel of the Lord appearing consoles her in her sadness, promising to restore another and a better rod. And without delay, the pain of her fever ceasing shortly after, the angel as she felt gently placed a stick about four feet long upon her breast and retired. And taking it with outstretched hand, in a certain sense she thought little of it; inasmuch as, twisted in appearance and heavy in thickness, it was far from the lightness

weak eyes of the sufferer from the glare of the summer sun, they made a roof for her bed with planks, drew the curtains, and hurried away to save what they could of their burning property. One can imagine the suffocating heat from which poor Lydwine suffered that terrible day and the following night.

[1] July 23rd.

of the lost rod, nor would it be for her so light and manageable. Murmuring therefore at this, she said silently to herself: "Am I even now well content?" But what should she do, since she was as yet unaware of the virtue of the wood? She then asks Master John, her confessor, to go over to a carpenter, and ask him to shape this stick with a plane to the form of a yard measure. The priest therefore enters the house of a certain artisan, who of his many tools had scarcely one plane fit for this work, the rest having been already burnt in the city fire. And when he had commenced to shave the wood, and had set his instrument well into it, such an odour of sweetness evaporated therefrom, and within it was bright with so fair a colour after the fashion of wax, that although outwardly it seemed ugly, nevertheless without hesitation he declared that it was cypress. Whereat both wondering, since the priest could not tell the carpenter of what kind was the wood or whence it had come to the virgin, they eagerly seized upon the shavings and other pieces cut off. Then, by the advice of the carpenter, the priest went with the unpolished wood to another better workman, that he might finish it off to a nicer shape. But when between them they remarked in wonder the same concerning the odour and colour of the unknown wood, and for reverence and the strangeness of the thing appropriated the pieces cut off, the priest in astonishment, not suffering the wood to be further lessened, carried it back in haste to the virgin. And when he had asked her whence it had come to her, and of what kind it was, she confessed that she did not know its species; but she told the priest how she had obtained it. Afterwards, however, on the feast of St. Cyriacus, martyr,[1] the angel coming back led her as usual to the gardens of Paradise, and, reproaching her for her little esteem of the rod, very clearly showed its worth and its place and the tree whence he had broken it. Then, coming back to herself, she narrated in order to her confessor what she had learnt of the angel, grieving that she had caused it to be cut down. When therefore the news of this sweet-smelling wood began to be noised abroad, and many were wishful to see and touch it, and because of it the

[1] Aug. 8th.

modest virgin suffered many visits, it happened that on account of the touch of a certain man,[1] the aforesaid wood lost the fragrance of its most sweet odour. And thereupon the virgin grieved that it had been shown to another, because of whose contact the heavenly odour evaporated. But she was wont to say that the devil would be chastised by this rod, as she had learnt from the holy angel.[2]

CHAPTER VI

OF THE BEREAVEMENT OF THE HEAVENLY BRIGHTNESS ON ACCOUNT OF ANOTHER HIDING IN HER CELL

On another occasion a kinsman of this virgin, Nicholas by name, went in to visit her with her confessor, and after they had had some conversation the modest virgin made known to them that she would like to be alone in her cell for two

---

[1] We learn elsewhere that this man was a libertine.

[2] In effect this rod was afterwards found most efficacious in exorcising persons possessed.

or three hours. She asked them therefore to go out for a walk for a time, hoping that in their absence, on account of her interior recollection, she would receive some special grace.[1] But in particular she asked Nicholas not to return before three or four hours. While therefore he did as she requested, the virgin's confessor without her knowledge secretly entered her cell. The virgin therefore, thinking that she was alone in the secret of her chamber, at once began to make herself ready to receive the grace of the heavenly spouse by devout prayers knocking at the inner gates of Heaven. And about half an hour after midday the angel of the Lord came in to her, flying around the place of the bed where the sick maiden lay, but he did not draw nearer to her. The virgin then, seeing that she could not enjoy his gladsome presence, being troubled, wept bitterly. She asked the angel, therefore, whether she had

---

[1] This reminds one of what is related by the Ven. à Kempis himself. Conversing sometimes with the brethren in recreation, he would suddenly break off, and with the remark, "Someone awaits me in my cell," gently take leave of them to entertain himself alone with Jesus.

offended the Lord by any fault whereby she had not deserved to enjoy this grace. But he answering, "By no means," said he, "but on account of the presence of him who is secretly seated in thy cell, and strives to examine and experience the grace prepared for thee." Having said this, the angel departed from her. Then the virgin, deprived of so happy a solace, was exceedingly saddened, and began to weep most bitterly, so that for a time she was not rapt in ecstasy, although she often enjoyed the grace of the angel's visit.[1] Her confessor therefore, hearing her weep thus, rising, told her that he had been present. And learning this, she was the more distressed than if another had been there, because she had so often revealed her life to him, so that without any spying he might believe the divine grace which was wrought in her. When therefore she had recovered from this trouble, and had regained her peace, the loving and compassionate Lord, as He had often

---

[1] The sense seems to be that, on account of the sadness, so intense as not to be without some imperfection, to which the servant of God gave way on this occasion, for some time afterwards she was not favoured by a complete ecstasy.

done before, so also afterwards raised her in ecstasy above herself. Then was fulfilled in her what is said by the psalmist: "Thou hast turned for me my mourning into joy: Thou has cut my sackcloth, and hast compassed me with gladness" (Psalm xxix 12).

CHAPTER VII

OF HER RAPTURE TO THE REGIONS OF PURGATORY, AND TO THE JOYS OF PARADISE, WHENCE SHE BROUGHT BACK A VEIL GIVEN HER BY THE BLESSED VIRGIN

After this she was rapt by the spirit who bore her to the regions of Purgatory, where, amid others whom she saw in manifold and grievous ways tormented, she saw also the souls of her friends punished, for whose deliverance and relief she afterwards cruelly afflicted herself in the body. When then she had seen with grief these purgatorial regions, and very many places of punishment wherein the souls were tortured according to the diversity of faults, God pitying her, she was led to contemplate the joys of eternal life. There indeed she saw how God Almighty enjoyed His own glory in Himself, according to that "I am the first and the last" (Is. xli 4), and "I will not give my glory to another" (Is. xlii 8); she saw also how the holy martyrs, confessors, prophets, virgins, and other orders of the blessed enjoyed their glory in themselves, and for overflowing delights were mutually transfused into one another. When she had gazed upon these joys, many saints addressing her sweetly comforted her and, exhorting her to patience, spake thus: "What trouble or harm is it to those who are here now, that in the world they suffered many adversities for Christ?" Then the most blessed Virgin Mary approached her in great glory, and kindly addressing her, questioned her, saying: "Why, most dear daughter, hast thou come with head uncovered and unadorned?" Then this virgin replied: "Most dear Lady Virgin Mary this is the will of the Lord and my God, and thus my conductor brought me here." After many familiar colloquies then of the Mother of God with this virgin, the time coming wherein she should return to her bodily senses, Christ's

Mother addressed these words to her: "Most dear daughter, do manfully, and let thy heart be strengthened in the bearing of sorrows; because for these things, which thou sufferest now, thou shalt gain wondrous and great glory." The blessed Virgin also added, saying, "Wouldst thou have a veil upon thy head?" She replied: "I cannot here have a will of my own." When therefore she had looked to her angel guide, and he, seeing that she resigned her own will, had consented that she should accept; "Receive," quoth the Blessed Virgin, "this veil upon thy head, which cannot be upon earth save for seven hours. Give it also into the hands of thy confessor; and tell him that I require of him to believe the gifts of the almighty Son of God, and to place this veil upon the head of my image which is in the church." After this had taken place, the godly virgin returned to her bodily senses, exultantly giving thanks to God for a consolation so joyful. But she was not aware that she had received such a veil materially; until at length, by the impulse of chance or necessity, placing her hand on her head she drew down a flower-bearing veil;[1] which from its most sweet odour she recognised as placed on her by the hand of the Blessed Virgin, and almost until the seventh hour of her return she kept it by her. Now this veil was of a yellow or golden colour, and of a texture hitherto unseen by mortal eyes; and it sent forth from itself an odour of wondrous sweetness, and therefore as long as she could she retained so beautiful and resplendent a veil by her. And so before the seventh hour she bade them rouse her confessor, and bring him to her speedily, having some secret things to relate to him. Who coming, asked her what she desired. To whom the virgin answered, that she had been present at a certain feast, and that the Blessed Virgin Mary had given her this veil, to bring to earth and place in his hands; that thereby he might believe the gifts of God, and by order of the Blessed Virgin receive this veil into his

[1] The word used throughout by the author is *sertum*, strictly, a *garland;* but other expressions in the description apply only to a *veil:* the key to the solution seems given by this clause *florigenum sertum*, signifying a combination of veil and garland such as is still the festive head-dress of peasant women in the Low Countries.

hands; and in the morning enter the Church which about that time had been burnt, and place it upon the head of the image of the Blessed Virgin Mary. And when the confessor asked how he could enter the church, since it was not yet day, and the church would be closed, she answered him: "Going quickly, ask the sacristan to open the church for thee; for the time presses wherein this veil must be carried back thence whence I brought it down." Then he: "How shall I place the veil upon the head of the statue, which is set in so high a position?" The virgin answered: "In the great choir and in such a place you will find a ladder; taking it, go up and place the veil on the head of the statue of the Blessed Virgin." Then he, after receiving this sign, going out, asked the sacristan to rise quickly and open the church. Which when he had willingly done, the virgin's confessor finding the ladder in the place which she had indicated to him, took it with him to the statue and mounted. To whom the sacristan: "What do you want there?" The priest replied: "What I do thou canst not know now; but the Lord will grant that thou wilt know it hereafter." Taking little heed of this answer, the sacristan, because he was not aware of the mystery, at once departed. But the devout confessor fulfilled the virgin's desire; and having placed the veil on the head of the sacred image, he carried back the ladder to its former position. When therefore he had prayed on bended knees before the statue, and reverently adored, and had fulfilled everything that had been commanded him, before he went forth from the church an angel of the Lord carried back the same flower-bearing[1] veil to its own place, whence the virgin had first brought it down: as she afterwards related to the aforenamed widow Catherine.

CHAPTER VIII

OF THE GLORIOUS CROWN PREPARED FOR HER, BECAUSE OF THE INSULTS AND WOUNDS INFLICTED ON HER BY THE MEN OF PICARDY[2]

Another time also, rapt in the spirit, she saw a crown exceeding glorious pre-

[1] *Florigerum.*

[2] *Stipendarii, quos vulgus Hollandiae Picardos vocat,* writes John Brugman, an expression which points to the conclusion that the general term for the mercenaries of the Duke of Burgundy was *Picardi,* here translated literally.

ST. LYDWINE *of* SCHIEDAM

pared for her, which she was to receive from the Lord after the toils and sorrows of the present life, wherein nevertheless there still seemed to be many things wanting. Coming back to herself therefore, mindful of the crown foreshown her, she begged the Lord with much urgency that in His compassion He would deign so to work with her that that crown might be perfectly completed. At the same time also she asked of the Lord, that in order to follow in His footsteps He would bring her to Himself, and after this union cast her forth with kicks. While she was constantly and most earnestly making this prayer, it happened in the year of the Lord 1425 that Philip, Duke of Burgundy, entered Holland with a large army of men from Picardy and other soldiers, to force the states to accept him as the master and ruler of the country. When therefore the most mighty duke had been received with honour in many cities, he came at length, about the feast of the holy martyrs Gereon and Victor,[1] to the town of Schiedam, where he was received in like fashion by the citizens. After the

---

[1] Oct. 10th.

refreshment of dinner, therefore, some, as it said, doctors and surgeons of the household of the aforesaid duke, approached Master John Angels the Curé of the Church and asked him to take them to the house of this virgin. Who, suspecting no ill of them, consented to their request. When then he had entered with them to the virgin, there followed a large body of their retainers, who behaved riotously; and as he strove to quell their uproar lest they should disturb the servant of God, they, throwing him aside angrily, bade him take himself off, uttering disgraceful words concerning his relations with her. The Curé therefore remained in her chamber standing near the altar, very sad and ashamed. Those perverse men, however, when they saw that she was lying in darkness, took away the curtain, lit a candle, and taking off the coverlet wherewith the dropsical virgin was covered, entirely stripped the holy maid, alas! revering neither God, nor the angels, nor the presence of men. This when the daughter of her brother, Petronilla, a young girl devoted to the service of the virgin, beheld, she bore it most ill; and on fire with the zeal of

God, bravely threw herself upon them, striving to protect the virgin's modesty. For she deemed it unbeseeming that the eyes of carnal men should behold naked the hidden gem of Christ. Then those wicked retainers, forgetful of decency, roughly seize upon this child, and casting her from them, violently dash her against the foot of the altar: so much so that most cruelly wounded on the thigh she was lame until death. Yea, and not satisfied with these evil deeds of violence, they hasten to others more grievous and criminal. For the holy and inviolate maid they dared to call a prostitute, they gabbled that she who lived abstemious and without food indulged in banquets by night, and one of them who held the light called her a beast, whom beyond doubt her angel guardian often carried off and led to Paradise. Amid these so many and outrageous words uttered by these impious men, they add disgraceful deeds, which the eyes of men would shudder to behold. For, casting off all shame, with their foul hands plucking and pinching the maiden feeble and greatly swollen in the skin on account of her dropsy, they wounded her in three places, from which the blood flowed so freely that it was necessary to drain off the fresh blood from the bed with a bowl. And after they had shamelessly committed this crime, going out they washed their hands of the blood which they had shed; and coming back, instead of the words for forgiveness which they should have implored, they again loosed their accursed tongues unto words of outrage. And thus was accomplished in this virgin what the Lord said to the disciples: "If they have persecuted Me they will also persecute you, and if they have called the good man of the house Beelzebub, how much more them of his household?" (Jo. xv 20; Matt. x 25). Then the virgin, lying as an innocent sheep upon her bed, bathed in her own blood, ready for the slaughter, patiently accepted all this for Christ's sake, and to them that insulted and wounded her she meekly answered with these words: "Why have you not fear to interpret the works of the Godhead in me so evilly; ye who know not what kind of judgment shall be yours from God?" The duke departing the same hour, those invaders also follow. But the magistrates of the city, hearing that such enormous injuries had been done to the virgin, as if for comfort of the ill done, threatened that they would lodge a complaint with the duke, that he might exercise just vengeance against the authors of so great a crime. Then the virgin, mild and patient in adversity, mindful of the word of the Lord, "Revenge to Me, I will repay" (Rom. xii 19), absolutely forbade them to wreak human vengeance, for God will speedily avenge this wrong. Which by the divine will quickly came to pass, for they all died in different parts the same winter. For one of them, who had held the light [1] and had uttered insults against the virgin, going on board in the harbour by Rotterdam, driven as by a violent wind from one part of the ship to another, was drowned by the prince of darkness and drawn out dead with a broken neck: he was buried in the cemetery. The second going mad near Zerix, lest he should

---

[1] Thrice the author refers to this matter of holding a lighted candle over Lydwine's bed, because of the peculiar cruelty of this action, since the virgin's sight was so weakened that her one remaining eye could endure no material light, Part I, Chap. VII, and that it even bled in the presence of such light, according to John Brugman.

injure those who were with him was thrown from the ship into a skiff, and, taken out dead, was buried in the city. The third, a soldier, perished wounded in battle. The fourth, who called himself a doctor, attacked by apoplexy at Slusa, became dumb. Whereupon, reminded by his servant of what he had done with others against the virgin, and asked whether he was sorry for the same, showing some sign of repentance to his questioner by touch of the hand and movements of the mouth, he died. And his servant coming afterwards to the virgin, with tears besought and obtained forgiveness for his master. The holy virgin therefore wept long over these injuries, not grieving for her wounds, but for their perdition and the crimes committed. And while the magistrates of the city stood near her, the virgin foretelling the future said to them, "I indeed have now suffered these things, but a judgment threatens you of which you are unaware." And not long after when some of them, charged as betrayers of the city, feared to be punished by the duke with death, they said: "Lo this is the judgment which Lydia foretold would befall us." After this the holy angel of the Lord, appearing to her and calling her sister, made known, that by the shameless violence done her by the men of Picardy she had been set in the footsteps of the Saviour as she had before besought, and by the outrageous words which she had heard from them, the jewels which remained were now completely finished in her crown.

CHAPTER IX

OF THE PATIENCE AND DEATH OF PETRONILLA, THIS VIRGIN'S NIECE

It is now befitting to relate something also of the maiden Petronilla, this holy virgin's niece. This young maid then of seventeen years of age was the daughter of the virgin Lydia's brother, a lover and guardian of perpetual chastity, taking care of her aunt day and night in the so grievous trouble of a long sickness. In the flesh a relative, in the spirit a sister, by service a handmaiden, she chose to serve the virgin as a virgin, and with chaste attentions to soothe most lovingly the pains of the sufferer. In the persecution of the men of Picardy, who most grievously wounded holy Lydia, the virgin pleasing to God, thereby to be crowned with more ample glory, with all her strength, as was said above, she set herself for the defence of her ailing aunt, that they might not harm the innocent one. For she grieved exceedingly with her who was injured, and hearing many grievous insults and threats, received and endured bodily wounds also from the men of Picardy, so that after ailing a long time she died of her injury. A few days before her death Lydia, set in great tribulation and from persecution rendered more fervent towards God, had the following vision, a true presage of what was to come. For on a certain night being in an ecstasy she saw a solemn procession of the heavenly citizens, wherein they each proceeded in distinct orders, to wit, the patriarchs together, the prophets together, the apostles with the apostles, but also the martyrs, confessors and virgins, and priests and clerics each shone in the rank and dignity of his state. And they proceeded from the church of the town of Schiedam, preceded as usual by crosses and lights burning more brightly than the sun, and they came to the door of her house, from which taking a coffin they bore it to the church. And the virgin herself followed the bier with crowns which had been given her, of which she bore one on her head, the others one in each hand. Coming back to herself therefore, she suspected that her own death was foreshadowed by this vision, but at length she said that it signified the death of her niece Petronilla. Whereupon the virgin of Christ, fearful concerning the passing away of her niece, urgently besought the Lord that He would so order her fevers that she might be able to speak to Petronilla for her comfort before her departure, for she loved her exceedingly with a sincere love. And the Lord, hearing her prayers and groanings and in pity for the one who was about to die, forestalled the time of the daily fever by the space of about six hours, to the surprise of many who were there, and thus the heat of the fever being cooled, she recovered power to speak with and console Petronilla, who was shortly to pass from the struggle of this world to Christ. Having received then divine comfort from the holy virgin, the maid Petronilla, after being often tried in anguish, as she was the companion of the sufferings of Lydia in life, so also she merited to be the sharer of her comfort in death. Therefore after the vision shown before, and having gratefully received consolation from her most dear aunt, the devout virgin of Christ, Petronilla departed to enter the heavenly court, in the year of the Lord one thousand four hundred and twenty-six, on the nineteenth of the Kalends of February, the feast of St. Pontianus, martyr.[1]

CHAPTER X

OF THE WITHDRAWAL OF DIVINE CONSOLATION, WHICH THE VIRGIN SUFFERED ON ACCOUNT OF HER GRIEF FOR HER DEAD NIECE

After the death then of the most chaste dove the maiden Petronilla, the holy virgin Lydwine herself, bereaved of the companionship of so faithful and neces-

---

[1] Jan. 14th. This Saint is distinct from St. Pontianus, Pope and Martyr, whose feast is celebrated Nov. 19th.

sary a helpmate, fell into a hurtful sadness, grieving too much for the loss of her most cordial lover Petronilla, with whom bound by mutual love, she had kept a compact of inviolable chastity. For, loving one another in the love of Christ, they lived together in such union and peace that they could not be separated from one another without grievous sorrow. Which fond union indeed, exceeding the bounds of discretion, was even so displeasing to the Lord that, in vengeance for this undue sadness, the grief-stricken virgin was left without divine consolation until the feast of the Visitation of the Blessed Virgin Mary.[1] She wept therefore most bitterly, not only for the death of her lost niece, but more for the bereavement of her wonted grace withdrawn from her on account of the want of measure in her grief. And so to those who asked the cause of these tears, she answered her friends: "Why should I not weep, most dear ones? Lo! now for the last eleven years I have asked nothing of the Lord, but I have been able easily to obtain it; but now in suspense for so long a time, I receive no consolation at all, by a secret

[1] July 2nd.

and righteous judgment of God given forth against me." O terrible and unsearchable dispensation of God over the sons of men! Who turneth the sea into dry land and rose blossoms into absinthe, and from the right setteth on the left, humbling the exalted even to the earth. If, then, the Lord afflicted a virgin so tenderly loved by Him because she bewailed too intensely the lost presence of her faithful niece, how severely are those to be punished who foolishly lament for carnal friends and worldly companions. However, the Father of mercies and the God of all consolation was not unmindful of the tears of His servant Whom He had chosen from eternity, but after most bitter sorrow He restored to her the most sweet comfort of the Holy Ghost so often tasted in the times past. Therefore the virgin, desolate for a time and chastised by her Father, about the feast of the Visitation of the Blessed Mary, Virgin, received a wondrous and superabundant consolation of divine grace, continuing for nine or almost ten days in constant contemplation and savour of things divine and exultation of mind; and with such great sweetness was she bathed within that those who visited her marvelled, and perceived the scent of a most sweet odour without. When then they questioned whence came an odour of such sweetness, she, desirous out of humility rather to be silent than to reveal the secret, at length overcome by their importunate prayers because the Lord had made this known outwardly by manifest signs, answered that the grace of so inestimable an odour came from the heavenly courts, which grace, as she had merited habitually of old, so now also having been visited afresh, she brought back with her. In a like manner a few years before, at the death of her brother William Peters, she fell into a great sadness and became so heavy with grief that she said she had not known hitherto that she was still so human. Wherefore also a long time she was bereaved of her wonted nourishment of divine consolation, as was revealed to a certain devout solitary in the country of Egypt who had bravely entered the desert by her advice. Of whose holy life, well commenced and happily consummated, is narrated in the following chapter that which may give joy to hear.

CHAPTER XI

OF THE DEVOUT YOUTH GERARD, WHO HAD BECOME A HERMIT, AND OF THE PILGRIMS WHO VISITED HIM

There was a certain youth, by name Gerard, a native of the diocese of Cologne, urged by the desire of a solitary life. Hearing the repute of this holy virgin, he resolved to come to her first to unfold to her in person his purpose, and commend to her prayers the difficult path which he was about to enter, that by the aid of divine grace he might accomplish with saving perseverance the resolution which he had conceived in his mind. And coming to her, he made known to her the secrets of his heart. And she, piously rejoicing in his purpose, with prophetic spirit foretold that for the first three days of his entry into the wilderness he should suffer want, and then, urging him to constancy, she foretold that after the end of the third day he should receive refreshment from God. Which indeed afterwards came to pass in order. For on the evening of the third day he received a heavenly manna, God taking pity upon his toilsome way. But the three days foretold him by the virgin he went through with such constancy that he was ready, on account of her promise, to pass them even with danger of his life. After mutual conference then and recommendation in prayer and the compact of fraternal charity, the new recruit, entering upon the wars of a new combat, went forth from the presence of the virgin wisely instructed, henceforth never again to see his country and kinsfolk. Having wandered therefore through the northern parts, he enters upper Egypt, and, penetrating its deserts, he finds a cell set in a tree because of the wolves and ferocity of the wild beasts. And he had brought with him two companions, touched by the grace of the same solitary manner of life, who after a few days spent there returned, alas! to the former things; but Gerard, most constantly persevering in the purpose he had undertaken, with Christ as leader climbed the heights of contemplation. And so after nearly seventeen years passed in this vast solitude, it happened meanwhile that a

ST. LYDWINE *of* SCHIEDAM

certain bishop from the country of England came with two companions to visit the places of the Holy Land, and then went on with them to see the relics of St. Catherine, virgin and martyr, on Mount Sinai. Who, united by like devotion, mindful of the life of the holy fathers in Egypt, entered that land to seek whether perchance they should find any fathers of the hermit life. And when wandering hither and thither they had come even to its upper parts, they find a little cell built in a tree not far from the ground. And knocking at its door, they see in the door opened to them a man of angelic countenance indeed, but of body so stout that he would be deemed as one not mortified in the desert but brought up amid the luxuries of the world. When then they asked whence he lived, he answered that he was nourished by the grace of God alone. For he was wont to gather and eat the heavenly manna, which of old the children of Israel fed upon in the desert, which, coming down upon his cell from above, he took with giving of thanks. They asked also of him whether there were still found other men who lived without human food as also himself, to whom he replied thus: "In the country of Holland, in the city of Schiedam, there is a certain virgin, for many years divinely scourged by divers infirmities, who makes use of no bodily food, who also has arrived at such a height of perfection that she is long ahead of me a hundredfold in holiness of life and sublimity of contemplation. Whence also I much wonder, since I hear nothing of her passing away, what has happened her, because for long I have not seen her on the ladder of contemplation, while formerly we were frequently wont to be rapt together to the heavenly secrets, each on a separate ladder. For she, as by merit of life so also by excellence of contemplation, was wont to rise above me." Then this devout hermit asked the aforesaid pilgrims to visit this virgin in Holland before they returned to their own parts, and from his mouth put her these three questions. First, how many years he had passed in the desert; secondly, of what age he was then when he entered the wilderness; thirdly, what reason had befallen her that for long he had not seen her in the wonted contemplation. After this the pilgrims, much consoled and edified, bidding the hermit farewell, returned to Holland and Schiedam. Having entered, therefore, an inn of the town, they ask their host to lead them to the virgin's house. And set in her presence, they make known the cause of their coming and the person of the hermit who had sent them, begging that she reply to the questions put her. But she, preferring to lie hidden through humility than openly answer the questions, gave only this response to her questioners, as regards the time of the dwelling of the hermit in the solitude: "How could I know that? It is the Lord who knows." Then they, as reproving her, object, why should she wish to conceal the truth, since they asked these things not of themselves but from the mouth of the hermit. She answered, therefore, that he had passed almost seventeen years in the solitude. To the second, however, she said that he was nineteen years of age when he set out for the desert. To the third also she replied that she, living in the midst of men, was stained in divers ways, but that he, separated from men and living with the angels, kept his purity untouched. "Therefore it is not strange if he excels me in the height of contemplation." It is also said that the hermit assigned the reason of the withdrawal of grace in the virgin that she was wont to grieve too much for the death of her relatives. Which happened at the death of her brother, who had passed away in Schiedam about the same time as the above was related to these pilgrims by the hermit in Egypt. But the same most devout hermit of happy memory, a perfect despiser of earthly things and a sublime contemplator of heavenly secrets, passed away in the year of the Lord's Incarnation, one thousand four hundred and twenty-six, the twelfth day of the month of October. His death and passing to glory were revealed to the holy virgin by a vision. For, rapt into Paradise at the hour of his passing, she saw his soul, freed of the body, borne by angels to Paradise, and washed in a fountain so limpid that she seemed to be able to see its depth for nearly a mile.

CHAPTER XII

OF THE HAPPY DEATH OF MASTER WERMBOLD, PRIEST, THIS VIRGIN'S FAITHFUL FRIEND

Among many devout fathers and men versed in spiritual grace, at Utrecht in the days of the venerable lord bishop Frederick, was a certain priest of chaste life and zealous for souls, by name Wermbold, beloved of God and men, and known far and wide to many religious in the diocese of Utrecht and in the country of Holland. He was a native of a certain town of Holland near Goudam, and for many years he shone as director and confessor of the Sisters of the Third Order at St. Cecily in Utrecht. Who, deeply versed in the divine scriptures, often preached the word of God in the church, and, fervently watching in prayers and devout meditations for the purity of his heart he merited also to be visited from on high by frequent consolations and divine revelations. To the knowledge of this so famous a father, not by human information but by divine revelation, the holy virgin Lydwine, still living in poverty in a poor hut, attained in this manner. For when on the feast of the Lord's Annunciation[1] the aforesaid virgin, having completed barely half her illness, was rapt to contemplate the things of Heaven, it happened also that the most devout priest of Christ, Wermbold, was likewise raised at the same hour to behold heavenly things; and then from having this one and like contemplation, they both commenced divinely that mutual acquaintance which they had not had before. Wherefore the same venerable father, urged by an affection of pious devotion, wished to know also and see with the eyes of the body the servant of God, whom he had known already in the spirit. Coming in, therefore, to her little house where she lay sick, and beholding her misery wherewith she was burdened, as the Samaritan in the gospel he was moved with compassion towards her, and wounded to the heart with the arrow of pity. And without delay, after holy converse on God, he stretched out his hands to

[1] Lady Day is thus named elsewhere also in the writings of the Windesheimers.

works of charity. And first he gave her about thirty groats of Flanders to buy two linen coverings. Then the priest, set on fire with the spirit of God, entered the church, and, mounting the pulpit, made a discourse to the people, in which with harsh reproaches he chastised them as they deserved for their niggardliness and want of mercy, inasmuch as they did not succour God's ailing creature who was lying in such want and pain. And justly indeed did the eloquent priest speak with severity for the zeal of God, for tried virtue reproves the foolish. Afterwards, however, many moved to mercy by the inspiration of God, with a generous heart bestowed their alms on the holy virgin. This reverend father therefore, among other discourses of charity with the sick virgin, who then had accomplished about a half of her diseases, began to say to her that before Easter a revelation had somehow been made to him as if he were to pass to the Father before this Easter. To whom the virgin replied, that he would have to wait until the next Pentecost, and that again after Easter he should visit her. And how true was this saying the issue of the affair proved. For he died shortly after these words in the year of the Lord 1413, on the vigil of Pentecost, at the twelfth hour of midnight, on the third of the Ides of June, on which day was kept the feast of St. Barnabas, apostle.[1] And being dead, the devout and compassionate father Wermbold was detained from the sight of the glory of the divine countenance for nearly nine days, as was divinely revealed to this virgin. But when this venerable father was speaking with the virgin before his death, paternally consoling her, and when she complained somewhat that she was much burdened by the number of her infirmities, the priest responded, encouraging her to bear more and, as it were, foretelling that it would be necessary for her to embrace still greater endurance, inasmuch as perhaps she had barely fulfilled half the term of her sufferings. And this so befell as he foretold. For he said that she had set in Heaven a foundation very broad and wide, and that the superstructure to be built thereon could not be perfected in a

[1] June 11th.

short while. And the virgin lived after the death of this dear father twenty years in the great pains and many sufferings foretold her, whom God nevertheless consoled and strengthened with frequent raptures by the inspiration of the Holy Ghost and the visit of heavenly citizens.

CHAPTER XIII

OF HER DIVERS RAPTURES AND HER KNOWLEDGE OF THE STATE OF CERTAIN RELIGIOUS

And so this virgin, feeble in body, fervent in spirit, was very often rapt into ecstasy by excess of mind; but in her rapture it was not *rara hora et brevis mora* (rare hour and brief delay). Once a certain religious questioned her concerning her state and patience in her afflictions which she endured daily. To whom she replied that she was burdened very excessively and above her strength, and that, unless the loving Lord supported her with the staff of consolation, she might easily faint away under the weight of her sorrows. For she said that by the influx of the divine mercy almost every night for a long period of one hour or more she was rapt to behold things heavenly, by the delight of which she was so refreshed that all torment, even the most bitter, was rendered for her not only bearable but even pleasant. She was also rapt to the regions of Purgatory and to the tortures of Hell, that, seeing these horrible punishments, she might more easily endure present scourgings, and by interior compassion might willingly do penance for those who needed deliverance. In these and the like blissful raptures, for nearly thirty-four years lying on a bed of pain, she was visited and strengthened in spirit; but at times she was deprived of the divine raptures, as has been said, from certain causes. Finally, in His many dealings by contrary events, God trying her often humiliated her, and frequently visiting her raised her the higher. By occasion therefore of these raptures she knew many churches and monasteries of religious and the arrangement of places and the building of churches; religious persons also, whom she had never seen, she knew by name, and what divinely befell them she sometimes narrated to others.

She had said once to a certain Prior that she knew his monastery and church just as he did, and that at night while the brethren were sleeping she was wont to visit their dormitory, and that she used to see holy angels standing by the beds of the brethren.[1]

There was a certain youth, Henry by name, born at Hague, a town of the duchy of Holland, whom the virgin had never seen before, who, inspired by the grace of God, without the knowledge of his parents sought and obtained the habit of holy religion in the parts of Brabant near Diest. Whose father, named William, knowing not what had happened his son, came to the virgin perhaps to ask some questions. Who, at once addressed by her in his own name and surname, heard the virgin wishing all prosperity to his son, and rejoicing over the good things done to him by God. Whereupon he, wondering, demanded the reason of these congratula-

---

[1] We learn from Brugman that this monastery was St. Elizabeth's of Briel, for the canons of which Ven. Thomas à Kempis compiled this *Life*. The community was incorporated into the Congregation of Windesheim by the general chapter of 1406 (*Chron. Wind.*, Lib. II, c. 39).

tions. And she, adding joyous tidings to his astonishment replied that he had been clothed in the habit of holy religion in the aforesaid monastery.

There was also another religious, born at Dordrecht, but professed as a regular in Eymsteyn, who once entered the virgin's cell silently to visit her, whom she, calling by his own name, very graciously greeted. And although perhaps she had seen him once before, at that moment certainly she did not see him bodily.[1] Whereat also he, being astounded, asked whence she thus knew him, to whom she replying simply said, "The Lord hath granted." Let these two examples be enough for the moment. Brother Hugh, formerly Subprior in Briel, heard them from the mouth of those to whom they personally happened, and he remains as a witness of their truth.

[1] The reader must remember again that the servant of God had entirely lost the use of one eye and almost entirely of the other, and that she habitually lay in darkness.

CHAPTER XIV

OF THE APPEARANCE AND KNOWLEDGE OF THE ANGELIC BRIGHTNESS ABOUT HER

Clearly in this most approved virgin was fulfilled that which of old the Lord said to Moses and the children of Israel entering the land of promise. "Behold I will send my angel who will go before thee and keep thee ever, and be the guide of thy way" (Exod. xxiii 20). We read in many books of the saints of the appearance of angels, and now the like can be proved in this lowly virgin Lydia from the testimony of many religious. For she was visited most frequently by a holy angel; by whom also she was touched as worthy of his companionship and trusting in his protection, whom she knew as personally as a friend knows his friend. Likewise she knew also the angels of her confessors, and of others her acquaintance, and of many outsiders. And the same angel appeared to her under different forms: sometimes in the shape of a most beautiful man, always, however, with great brightness, as an angel of light, the minister and standard-bearer of eternal light. Sometimes, however, that brightness was so great that if a thousand suns together shone in their might, yet they would not be able to equal this angelic splendour. At times however he appeared less bright, but always he bore the standard of the Lord's cross upon his forehead, lest perchance she should be deceived by an angel of Satan, who, transfiguring himself into an angel of light, often appeared to her. If however on account of the frequency of visitors she was sometimes disturbed, or on account of the presence or contact of some unclean persons her purity was stained, lest this slight fault should remain long on the white fleece, or pass unpunished, she was deprived of the aforesaid angelic visits and divine raptures. Sometimes also she was burdened in her conscience with certain spiritual defects known only to God and the angels: by reason of these scrupulously chastised she was also hindered from her wonted raptures. Whereupon, bruised in the mortar of her heart, she was wont to confess to the holy angel her guide; and thus cleansed by a humble confession, she hastened to follow him as he went before to the places whither he led. She was also taught by the same holy angel what she ought to confess to him and what to her confessor, for she confessed her excesses daily, according to that word of the psalmist: "I said I will confess against myself my injustice to the Lord, and Thou hast forgiven the wickedness of my sin" (Ps. xxxi 5).

CHAPTER XV

OF THE WONDERFUL MANNER OF HER INTERIOR PAIN BEFORE THE RAPTURE OF HER SPIRIT

In that to us indescribable separation of the spirit from the soul, before the holy virgin was rapt out of herself, at first she felt such anguish in the vital parts of the breast and heart that, scarcely able to breathe, she thought she was about to die. But afterwards in these spiritual raptures, accustomed by habit she did not suffer so much pain. When therefore she was rapt in spirit to the aforesaid places, her body remained as dead and soulless upon the bed, so immovable that if anyone had touched it she would not have felt anything. Something similar is read in the life of St. Thomas of Aquin, so that no one should doubt of the truth of the novelty in this virgin, whom God rejoiced by His ineffable raptures.

It happened therefore in a certain rapture, that the angel having taken her hand led her to the altar of the chapel of the Blessed Virgin in the church of Schiedam. And when she had prayed there, devoutly greeting the Blessed Virgin, the angel led her towards the west by pleasant places of roses and lilies, and set with every kind of flowers and covered with spices. Approaching therefore these places, she was invited by the angel to enter but for reverence thereof she dared not enter, lest she should tread the flowery meadows with her feet. At length when the angel assured her that they would not be downtrodden by her, entering according to his counsel and invitation, she followed him whithersoever he went before. But at times those flowers were of such a height and density that she said she could not pass through them; and then the angel carried her over as of old Habacuc the prophet, so that lifting her he speedily carried her across with confidence through those flowers to the place whither they wended.

CHAPTER XVI

OF HER SPIRIT OF PROPHECY, WHEREBY SHE REVEALED TO OTHERS MANY HIDDEN THINGS

And it is certain that this virgin also knew many secrets concerning both the living and the dead, of which some she made known for the profit and comfort of her friends, but many she humbly kept back in silence. For instance she is believed to have long before foreknown the fire of the city of Schiedam, because before it happened she had ordered a store of planks to be set against the wall of her house. To those who asked why she did this she said, because if the fire broke out then they could more easily, having removed the planks, carry her out and bear her across the moat.[1]

[1] *i.e.* the little canal, or ditch that ran round the house. Another, and as it seems the true reason is given in Brugman's second *Life* for this storing of planks, viz. that a rough shelter might be made near her house for some of those who should be rendered homeless by the fire.

It happened then in the year of the Lord 1428 that certain sailors of Schiedam, before setting out for the fishing, carefully made ready a great supper for their comrades and friends to bid them farewell on the feast of St. Arnulph, bishop and confessor, rejoicing indeed in present prosperity, fearing nothing of the evils to come. When therefore, having finished their supper, they had covered the fire under a vessel near a wall of reed, then lo! about the eleventh hour of the night gradually a fire breaks out, which, raging for the rest of the night, made such way that nearly the whole city with the church and the house of the sisters near the church was burnt. When this had come to pass, very many men of that city held it for certain that this great fire had befallen because of the sins of certain individuals, who amongst other crimes had shown irreverence to the aforesaid image of the Blessed Virgin Mary. Among whom was a woman worldly and unrestrained, following the broad paths of this world with the dissolute. After whose death a certain priest well known to this virgin asked her to pray for him, that he might have some certain knowledge of the state of the dead woman. And when the virgin agreed and did accordingly, the same priest, in a vision of the night rapt to the infernal regions, saw that the aforesaid woman was held bound with iron chains in hell, which also he related to this virgin with wonder and grief.

CHAPTER XVII

OF A CERTAIN DEPARTED SACRISTAN AND MANY OTHER DEAD

There was a certain sacristan Baldwine by name, in the town formerly called Oudershie, who falling sick died on the night of the Conversion of St. Paul,[1] and whose name this virgin did not know before. But the same night the virgin, absorbed in prayer, rapt as usual from her senses, came to a certain mountain, at the foot of which she saw a man then unknown to her wishing to climb the mount, but for weakness not able. And when according to his request placing him on her shoulders she had carried him up, wondering at his weight she

[1] Jan. 25th.

asked by what name he was called. Who answering said, "Baldwine de Velde." The next morning Master John the virgin's confessor, entering her cell, found her breathing heavily as from weariness of a great labour and from fatigue scarcely able to draw her breath. The priest therefore asked the cause of this distress and weariness. And she explained in order the thing shown in the vision, and told the name of the man before unknown that he was called Baldwine. Whereat wondering, that priest recalled to mind the sacristan at Oudershie, who was called Baldwine, but his surname he did not know. After two days the same priest came to that town to celebrate, asking a certain woman about the condition and surname of the same sacristan, who gave his surname as it was revealed to the virgin, declaring likewise that he died on the same night on which the virgin had carried him from the foot of the mountain to the top.

Another time also, rapt as usual, she came by a certain mountain and she saw divers persons wandering in different ways, some at the foot of the mount, others struggling higher up, and some standing on a more lofty part of the mount, wishing indeed to climb the mountain itself but unable and not having either any assistance to aid them. The virgin therefore understood what these things signified, that they were souls of the departed who needed prayers.

And when some of the solemn festivals were at hand, for some days before those feasts she would be rapt to the regions of Purgatory, to see the miseries of the afflicted who needed help and were unable to assist themselves, that she might faithfully pray the Lord for them, who, tormented with most grievous pains, were forced to cry out with Blessed Job, "Have pity on me, have pity on me, at least you my friends, for the hand of the Lord hath touched me" (Job. xix 21). Returning to herself, therefore, when she had willingly borne her daily fevers for their deliverance and most bitterly wept imploring urgently the divine mercy, again in rapture on the feasts themselves she exulted with such great gladness over their redemption, which she learnt, that she could scarcely hold herself in for joy. And although on other days she often liberated great numbers, still on the chief festivals by the favour of God she delivered many more and in greater abundance. But she so bitterly grieved over their sufferings and frequently wept that, natural tears failing in her, tears of blood succeeded, which, congealed in course of time upon her cheeks, her confessor scraped off, softening them with the natural tears that flowed, and placing them in a bag he kept them by him in a casket, and after her death, as she wished, placed in the tomb under her head.

CHAPTER XVIII

OF HER CAUTION AND PRUDENCE CONCERNING THE REVELATION OF THE STATE OF THE DEPARTED

Very cautious and circumspect was this virgin speaking of the state of the departed, although very often she was not unaware of the secrets of God. Which from the following example will appear from her words as a warning for the inexperienced, whom visions of the dead often deceive. After the death then of William Duke and Count of Holland and Zeeland, under whom this virgin flourished and long lay sick, a certain popular rumour was noised and came to the ears of the Countess Margaret, wife of the Duke now dead, that this virgin had said that he was already saved. She had also heard that this virgin had been dead for three days and had come to life again. The noble and venerable lady then sent one of her servants to her, to inquire into the truth of this affair. Being questioned therefore on each point by the messenger sent, she thus replied to the one: "If I had been dead three days the people of Schiedam would long since have buried me." But to the other, as she deemed the question absurd, she replied after a fashion saying: "If he were already in eternal life then the Lord would be doing me a wrong, who, held down for seventeen years by most grievous maladies, have not left my bed or touched the ground. Wherefore I beg that you do not sin by occasion of me." And thus the messenger who came uncertain returned thence more uncertain. However, of several departed religious she sometimes gave certain information, that they were saved and brought into the joy of their Lord. But of the last days and the coming of Antichrist she used to say that she herself would see neither of these.

CHAPTER XIX

OF THE TEMPTATION OF A CERTAIN MAN, DELIVERED BY THE ADVICE OF THE VIRGIN FROM THE SNARE OF THE DEVIL

A certain citizen, an honourable man and a counsellor of the town of Schiedam, was grievously tempted by the devil to cast violent hands upon himself by hanging himself. But he had a priest and a good chaplain, John by name, adorned by the grace of God, who was wont to celebrate Masses before him, and pray for him. As often then as he knew him to be tempted he could scarcely persuade him not to inflict a cruel death upon himself. But since he could not resist the violence of the temptation and his confessor could not keep back the tempted man from the rope, the priest, very anxious because of the danger, came to the virgin for advice and asked what he should do with the tempted man. Then she, knowing that the devil could not bear that the arts of his malice should be turned into arms of salvation, counselled the priest that if the tempted man could not resist the suggestion of the devil he should place upon him as a penance that which the evil enemy suggested for his ruin. Hearing which the confessor, fearing lest he should be the cause of his perdition, did not dare tell the tempted man what he was advised. But she, trusting in God, bade him do it with all confidence in his conscience. When then on one occasion, the priest finding an opportunity, did with the tempted man as the virgin advised, the tempted one gave thanks on bended knees that now at length he merited to obtain what he had so long desired. And at once returning home, fastening a rope to a beam and passing it round his neck he mounted a seat, that being tied he might hang himself. But, O wondrous clemency of God and unspeakable providence of divine mercy Who turned the snares of the devil unto the deliverance of His servant on account of the obedience of the priest consenting to the advice of the virgin of Christ. The demons therefore, seeing and grudging that he should depart by such a death, violently seizing him with the rope and snatching him away, said, "You shall not hang yourself now." And being furiously enraged they threw him and forced him down behind a chest, between the wall and the chest. And after being much sought for by his servants for the space of nearly three hours, and at length found there to the great astonishment of all, he was drawn out only by the removal of the chest, and thereafter he remained freed from that temptation.

CHAPTER XX

OF A WOMAN FREED BY THE MERITS OF THE BLESSED VIRGIN MARY FROM THE GULF OF DESPAIR

In the city of Schiedam was a certain woman timid and fearful whom the devil had almost cast into the abyss of despair. For he very often put before her during sleep a sheet with a certain sin formerly committed by her, as if not yet forgiven by God nor to be forgiven, although nevertheless she had very often confessed it sacramentally, had received absolution, and had performed the penance enjoined. She often therefore exposed the anguish of her heart to this virgin, and she comforted the desolate soul with loving counsels, and nevertheless did not succeed with her as she would have desired, because the prince of death troubled her as before in sleep with ever fresh terrors, saying: " By no means shalt thou be able to escape my hands, for by these letters I have thee confirmed and subject to me." It happened therefore on one occasion that the virgin, engaged in prayer, rapt to Heaven, saw the demon carrying this very document in his hand, but by the hand of the Blessed Virgin Mary it was violently taken away and snatched from his hand. For the merciful Lady was able to destroy all the machinations of the devil; and to comfort the sad soul with the trust of a good hope. These things afterwards the virgin, restored to her bodily senses, related to her confessor John Walters, showing that the devil's malice was frustrated by the compassion of the Blessed Virgin. After this the aforesaid woman as before laid the complaints of her desolation before the virgin; whom she, gently consoling, without mentioning however the destruction of the paper, bade to be henceforth secure, nor to fear any evil would befall her thereby. Yea and offering herself a hostage for her conscience on the day of judgment and trusting through all in the divine mercy, she rendered her free and at rest from all the former fear.

CHAPTER XXI

OF HER GRACE OF GREAT COMPUNCTION AND ABUNDANT SHEDDING OF TEARS IN THE COMMUNION OF THE BODY OF CHRIST

Now next something must be said of the state of this most devout virgin, as regards the holy Communion; how by the breathing of divine grace she gradually made progress to higher gifts by frequently receiving the sacraments of the precious body of Christ. At that time therefore of her dryness, when the virgin, as yet unacquainted with spiritual sweetness, lay sick upon a bed of most bitter sorrow, there was a certain devout priest named Master John Pot who was accustomed to communicate with her twice a year, and who first formed her to meditation on the Lord's Passion. He therefore, having a care for the salvation of the sick maiden, when one day he was about to communicate her, taking in his hands the sacred and spotless host he bade her very gravely and feelingly to look upon and receive Him Whom he held in his hand, knowing for certain that He was the Lord God her Creator Who had been made flesh, suffered and died for her, Who would also most abundantly recompense her for every affliction which she bore and would soften every pain. By which words she was at once exceedingly touched, and as it were wounded by certain fiery darts of love. And as before for grief of heart and impatience of feeling she could not cease from many tears, so also now for almost a fortnight or more she could not withhold her weeping for greatness of contrition and divine love. For she grieved and wept much over the blindness of her past negligence and her continued dullness, in which she had been so long impatient and thoughtless that she could not receive the consolation of her mother or of any man nor tell the cause of her tears to any. Now henceforth, having received the saving sacrament with great contrition, she commenced to be refreshed with frequent divine consolations, although she did not yet go into ecstasy by the rapture of contemplation. And nevertheless she did not wish to make known the reason of her tears to those who questioned her, that she might not lose the hidden manna which she tasted, but might keep it in her heart the more safely by silence. And she enjoyed these consolations by divine dispensation for about eight years before she began to be rapt in ecstasy out of the senses of her body. With these two aids then, to wit, the holy Communion of the body of Christ and devout meditation on the Lord's Passion, as by two loving arms she embraced her beloved spouse Jesus Christ; and therefore she could confidently say with the spouse in the canticle of love, whose grace of ineffable sweetness she frequently felt in herself by experience: "A bundle of myrrh is my beloved to me, He shall abide between my breasts" (Cant. i 12). For as myrrh preserves the bodies of the dead from rottenness, so also the daily exercise of the passion of Christ preserved her mind from impatience and murmur. And as material bread strengthens him who eats, so the receiving of the body of Christ refreshing her spirit brought her life and joy.

CHAPTER XXII

OF HER INSATIABLE DESIRE TO COMMUNICATE OFTEN, AND OF THE APPEARANCE OF A CHILD CRUCIFIED

When our Saviour Jesus Christ was preaching the gospel of the kingdom of Heaven, among many heavenly words which He taught He uttered this most saving word of faith concerning the sacrament of His body. " He that eateth Me, the same also shall live by Me " (Jo. vi 58); to wit, eating Me either spiritually only, or also sacramentally and spiritually: or certainly he shall live now in the life of grace, and hereafter in the life of everlasting glory reigning with Me; for this the sacred Communion of My body and blood signifies. Which faithful promise was undoubtedly fulfilled in this virgin, Christ most lovingly working His wonders in her. For although through nearly the first half of the period of her maladies she used very little nourishment and such as could not support nature, as is related in the first part of this book, and moreover although for all the rest of her life she took almost no food or drink at all, nevertheless this holy servant of God could not entirely abstain from this living food and life-giving sacrament of the body of Christ. For as much as she languished by corporal infirmities in the body, and took less bodily food, so much the desire of the heavenly and divine food increased in her, and by means thereof she was strengthened in spirit and lived more spiritually within. Whence in the beginning of her sickness for three or four years she was wont to communicate once a year at the feast of Easter, but afterwards with the beginning of the divine consolation for some years she received Christ twice a year. After that, when her mother was dead, so much did her desire increase, and so much was she drawn to communicate, that six times or more she received the Lord's body with full faith and special devotion unto the singular solace and assistance of her soul; and she would have received the same more frequently if the Curé of the church had not refused her. Whence also, if sometimes she asked to receive the holy Communion of the body of Christ from him, very grudgingly and against his will he would come to her, over which she grieved much. For the longer she lay in her sickness the more she suffered and languished in the body, and the more she suffered in the body the more she burned in divine love, and the more she was on fire with divine love so much the more the grace of Almighty God worked in her.

After this a certain wondrous vision appeared to the virgin, on fire with the desire of communicating. For a certain visible likeness of a crucified Child[1] with five wounds appeared to her lying in bed, which afterwards changed into a sacramental host with the same wounds hung in the air over the sheet of her bed, wherewith the virgin was in part

[1] John Brugman informs us that on this occasion the Saint received the *Stigmata*, but that at her request these signs of the divine favour were concealed by the partial covering of the wounds, which nevertheless continued to cause intense pain.

covered. She sent therefore a messenger to the Curé of the church that he should come to her, and see Christ appearing to her in a host, which also certain others saw with their own eyes. Then she begged him to give her this host in Communion and not to distrust her and the works of God. Hearing this, although doubtful, he gave her the host of the vision, which the virgin begged to receive and received with reverence.[1] After the wondrous appearance of this host and its devout reception the heart of the virgin was inflamed with so great a divine love and desire for holy Communion, that for many years she received the venerable sacrament of the Eucharist every fortnight from the hand of the priest, who also was obliged to use for this great care and foresight, for otherwise she would not have been able to consume it for weakness. Afterwards, however, he would offer her a little water for the ablution, wherein, little as it was, she suffered such difficulty in her throat that she could scarcely swallow it. But

[1] The author discreetly passes over in charitable silence the disgraceful behaviour of the Parish Priest on this occasion.

sometimes he gave her no ablution, on account of the too great difficulty of receiving it. And this state as regards her communion endured indeed until the year of the Lord 1421. But from this time until her death she commonly suffered her quartan and sometimes daily fevers for the freeing of souls from Purgatory. During which period she burned with so great a divine love that usually, when at the time of the quartan fever she was not suffering a fever attack, she communicated from the hand of her confessor two days following. And this holy and venerable sacrament of the body of Christ was for the sick virgin, not only the spiritual refreshment of her soul, but also a certain relief and support of her afflicted body. Especially, however, at the time of the withdrawal of grace and bereavement of divine consolation she received this most sacred banquet of the Lord's body more frequently as her singular support. For the interior grace of divine consolation, which she very often felt in abundance of spirit and joy of heart, was to her refreshment of body and soul; and again, by its absence her body was so weakened that without spiritual

ST. LYDWINE *of* SCHIEDAM

nourishment she could scarcely subsist and live in the body. Therefore, as has been said, she burningly thirsted for the body of Christ and received it as the support of life, lest she should die of weariness under the burden of suffering in the present pilgrimage. In the receiving of which she was frequently illumined with so great a divine light, that as with the bodily eyes she saw materially, so also, bathed with this supercelestial light, she saw all her interior with the eye of the mind. This same thing also befell her at other times in the presence of the divine light and the rapture of the contemplative life. Whence also afterwards, in the time of her dryness and the withdrawal of consolation, when by divine ordinance she did not experience this illumination, she would say within herself: " O where are now those days in which I was wont to behold my interior with the interior eye, as with the eye of the body I saw bodily things?" And thus was fulfilled in her that saying of the Wise Man: "In the day of good things be not unmindful of evils; and in the day of evils be not unmindful of good things" (Eccl. xi 27).

CHAPTER XXIII

OF THE FEVER OF THE CHILD BALDWINE, AND OF MASTER JOHN HER CONFESSOR

Now the desolate virgin had with her for some comfort in the latter days of her illness the son of her brother, by name Baldwine, a child of twelve years, almost continually waiting upon her. And that he might remember more surely the wondrous things that were wrought in her, and which he beheld by frequent experience, she obtained for him from the Lord the malady of a fever by a wholesome affliction and a certain loving miracle as a reminder of His wonders. For the same young lad used a certain cup from which she was wont to drink. And so about the feast of the birth of the Blessed Virgin Mary,[1] in that year before the day of her death, the virgin when it was now evening bade the same child to place his cup filled with a light liqnor near her bed. When morning came, calling the child, she bade him take the cup and drink. When therefore he had taken the cup

[1] Sept. 8th.

he found it by the gift of God filled with a certain strange liquor, as if there were in it a concoction made of a mixture of cinnamon and other simples sweet smelling and delicious to the taste. But as this virgin, according to the multitude of afflictions wherewith she was daily scourged, was also refreshed with divine consolations, so on the other hand the aforesaid child, having received and drank as much as he would of the aforesaid cup, on the same day began to languish and to be troubled successively with divers fevers until about the feast of St. Martin, bishop, in the winter time of the same year.[1] But from the same miraculous cup divers men also drank, but they did not however contract any maladies as the aforesaid child. Likewise also different liquors poured into the same cup for a whole week gave to those who drank the savour of a most sweet potation, without the affliction of any disease. This cup then, which to the child was a sign of scourging, to others who tasted was the solace of a fresh miracle. But when the child was cured of his fevers, the hand of the Lord was again stretched out to the

[1] Nov. 11th.

priest of this virgin. For Master John her confessor fell into quartan fever, and on the same day on which the virgin was usually attacked, he also being struck suffered a severe fever. Seeing this, Master John's sister asked the virgin how long the fever of her brother was to last. Who answered that he would be freed about the first Sunday of the following Lent, which also so came to pass as she foretold. And when the same Master John was sick with a serious illness unto death, the virgin, compassionating him, by the great urgency of her prayers mercifully obtained for him from the Lord delay of death and lengthening of life.

CHAPTER XXIV

OF HER SUFFERING FROM STONE AND HER FOREKNOWLEDGE BEFORE THE DAY OF HER DEATH

The Virgin of Christ, Lydwine, after being tried in many pains that there might not remain in her the stain of sin, at length with still another most sharp affliction was stricken and cleansed. In the last year of her life therefore, from the feast of the Purification[1] unto the feast of the following Easter, together with the other maladies which she had before for a very long time, she was afflicted with such a pain of the stone, that two or three times, lying as almost dead for nearly an hour, she could not speak. And she endured this suffering with a most intense toothache without any expression of impatience, and at its barely ceasing she was just able to utter only a very few words. And she said that the same stone, which was about the size of a pigeon's egg, would cause her death.

At that time also she was so seldom visited of God by interior consolations that she complained to Master John her confessor with tears that she was in a certain manner abandoned by the Lord beyond all wont. In which desolation, however, greater merit was added to her by her patience, because she was rendered more like to Christ suffering on the cross, Who with a loud voice called to the Father, saying, "My God, My God, why hast Thou forsaken Me?" (Matt. xxvii 46). And this holy virgin, as a true lover and bearer of the cross, per-

[1] Feb. 2nd.

severed and endured her maladies unto death, which also she had foreknown long before by a revelation from the Lord. For when a certain religious Prior called by her had come to her, to wit, on the feast of the Chair of St. Peter [1] the same year in which she died, the next day very early the same Prior was bidden by Master John the virgin's confessor to enter her cell if he wished to experience any spiritual favour in her regard. When then he had entered her cell he perceived therein such a fragrance of a most sweet odour which the virgin, then visited by the Lord and borne to the heavenly regions, had brought back with her, as if divers aromatic herbs had been scattered in the said cell. After mutual and divine converse then on those things wherefore she had summoned the Prior, she counselled him to return to her at Easter to confer still about these things in the best manner the Lord should grant. But if he should not find her, that then he should in charity pray for her. From which words it is clearly evident that she said this of her death, although she did not express any mention of death.

[1] Feb. 22nd.

CHAPTER XXV

OF THE GRACE ON EASTER NIGHT AND THE PROPHECY OF HER DEATH

And when the Easter solemnity arrived, on the holy night itself of the Lord's resurrection about the fourth hour of the breaking dawn, the aforesaid Master John her confessor came to see the virgin, and both from the scent of her hands and from her words he clearly perceived that she had been visited as usual by her holy angel. For he found such a sweetness upon her that she seemed to have been anointed with the oils of different spices.[1] Whereupon, when he gave thanks to the Lord and congratulated her, she, coming back to herself after this visitation, confessed that she had been divinely comforted, but declared that most grievous afflictions

---

[1] Brugman relates in his second *Life* that in this Easter vision Lydwine received Extreme Unction from the hands of Christ, quoting as his authority certain private revelations: "id ab eis accepi, quibus ipsa post mortem virgo devota Lydwine personaliter dignata est revelare." This would explain why the Saint, although she foreknew the hour of her death, made no request for this sacrament, but wished to die absolutely alone.

were about to befall her, which she would suffer during this festival. She also said that on the same night she had heard the Alleluia sung in the Heavens, and she hoped that she would shortly sing the same canticle Alleluia with the heavenly spirits in greater joy and consolation, and that she would suffer less from those maladies if the Easter festival were over. Which she seems to have said of the passing of her death, although she did not show that she was soon to die. But each day, to wit, on Easterday itself and the two following, she said to those who came to her that the pains which she was then suffering would not last long; as afterwards the issue proved.[1]

---

[1] There is another prophecy of her death which, although it appears in John Gerlac's German MS., was not inserted in Brugman's translation, and thus seems to have escaped our author. Some years before her death Lydwine related to her confessor and friends that her angel had shown her in Paradise a rose tree covered with buds, and had given her to understand that when all these roses were in full bloom the measure of her merits and her days of exile would be accomplished. From time to time her friends would ask how was it with her rose tree, and she would sadly reply that it was as yet far from its full flowering. But in the beginning of

ST. LYDWINE *of* SCHIEDAM

CHAPTER XXVI

OF HER HAPPY DEATH AND SUFFERINGS AT THE LAST

Therefore, when the Tuesday within the octave of Easter dawned, the virgin, mild and patient, wishing to recollect herself more fully, asked Master John her confessor, who came to her early, that neither he nor any of those who loved her should enter to visit her that day except the child Baldwine, who carefully waited on her unto death. Which also was done, that according to the desire of her heart she might die in solitude and forsaken of men. For the aforesaid her confessor related to a certain religious that, four or five years before her death, he had heard her asking the Lord, that she might die with none save Himself as witness and not without her own knowledge. And she had likewise begged that He would multiply her pains and infirmities, lessen

---

1433, answering the same question, she had joyously exclaimed: "Behold, all the roses are opened; it will not now be long before I die." The Saint is sometimes represented holding a bouquet of roses.

her days, hasten the hour of death, and render the agony brief; which also came to pass as will shortly appear. All the members of her household then having been dismissed, and in the absence of Master John, who was then saying the Office of the dead for a certain departed mother of the Sisters, the virgin approaching her end in the presence of only the aforesaid child, who held a bowl for her and carried out her vomit, she was so distressed in throwing up this vomit that to the child her attendant pitying her she said: " My most dear child, would that my Master John knew how much I am afflicted now." Nor is it strange if she confessed herself afflicted in these sufferings, when pain coming upon pain increased in her. For from the seventh hour of the same day in the morning, until nearly the fourth hour after midday before she died, she threw up about twenty times a very green matter, which she thought came from the bitterness of the gall. And when the aforesaid child, seeing and hearing these things, asked her whether she wished him to call Master John; at length with the coming of the last vomit, she suffered such difficulty in it that

ST. LYDWINE *of* SCHIEDAM

not being able to cast out the matter gathered in her throat, she commenced to choke with it. Seeing which the innocent child, thinking that she would die at once, weeping ran out and told this to Master John and the others of the household assembled there. And when likewise weeping they hastened thither, they found her in her agony. Then Master John, taking her hand, asked her for a sign whether she lived or whether she wished to be anointed. And when she made no reply, lighting a candle and setting it in a lantern, the priest placed the light behind her head, for he thought that she was still living, and therefore could not bear the light. He found that she was dead, and that she had escaped the wretchedness of the present life. But from the time when she last spoke until her expiry, scarcely the space of three *Misereres* intervened; and thus her end was seen to be short, as she had long before asked of the Lord. But the most patient virgin, pleasing to God and the angels, died on the twelfth of the Kalends of May, on the feast of SS. Tiburtius and Valerianus;[1] in the year of the Lord's incarnation 1433, on the Tuesday within

[1] April 14th.

the Octave of Easter about the fourth hour after vespers, in the fifty-third year of her age, which according to the cycle of festivals had been completed on the Palm Sunday before her death. And very befittingly, God arranging the order of seasons, she passed out of this world in Easter week; that she who had long been a sharer of the sufferings of Christ in meditation and compassion, might also with Him on the holy paschal feast of His most joyous resurrection pass to the bliss of eternal life. And the chosen virgin of Christ stricken by divers scourges of afflictions passed away, after accomplishing from the beginning of her maladies thirty-eight years, in the commencement of the thirty-ninth, being worthy to be associated with the choirs of angels, who from the years of childhood strove to imitate the life of the angels in chastity.

CHAPTER XXVII

OF THE WONDERFUL PLACING OF HER ARMS, AND THE SHROUDING OF HER BODY

And after her death certain marvels were discovered about her body, concerning which sure witness is possessed. For her right arm, which for many years had been so dead that she had not been able to move it by herself, but afterwards through a sharp operation by a certain surgeon it had become somewhat movable, after her death, when her holy body was uncovered, contrary to all hope and knowledge, no one knowing how it had come to pass, was found beseemingly lying with her left arm on her breast, with the hands as it were joined and the fingers bent. For she had been wont while still alive to say to some that she hoped that yet before her death she would praise God with both arms outstretched, which also came to pass and was clearly seen by many after her death. For many years also, and about thirty before her death, she used many hair girdles to chastise her flesh, girded with the last of which for about three years, she ended her last day. When therefore she was dead, and having been uncovered for the burial, was about to be clothed again, those who were there found the aforesaid girdle about her shoulders, loosed from her body in a manner unknown to men, but whole and round and not untied from the links of its fastening.[1]

She had also asked long before her death of the above named Master John her confessor that he would not suffer her after her death to pass a long delay upon the earth, but would at once see that she was clothed, and according to the manner arranged by her have her buried. And although he would willingly have done this, he was prevented by the violence of the magistrates of the city, whom he could not resist. For they had bidden him under penalty of his goods and body not to remove her from the place. The body therefore remained until the morning of Wednesday clothed in the wonted manner, and placed in a wooden chest, and set in the same place where it had lain for nearly twenty years in life. And the same venerable body was clothed after the fashion of religious sisters in a robe of wool, girded without by the hair girdle

---

[1] Michael d'Esne, Bishop of Tournai, in the beginning of the seventeenth century, says of this girdle: "It is still preserved, fragrant with a wondrous odour of sweetness. In fact I have handled it with my own hands, and I know by experience that the demons dread it exceedingly." *Quoted by Bollandists.*

which in life she had been wont to wear next the flesh. Then above her head was placed a round coif or a kind of circular mitre made of vellum, on the circle of which the glorious names Jesus and Mary were written with black ink, with which several hearts had been depicted as if transfixed with arrows or sharp darts. And all these things necessary for her burial she had prepared many years before, and thinking of her end she held them by her according to that word of the prophet, " Make ready to meet thy God, Israel, for the Lord shall come and He shall not be slack to render to each according to his works." But under her head, as she had desired, was placed a certain bag with her sweetly redolent tears of blood, which she had called roses, which from great charity and sorrow of heart had distilled from her eyes. These indeed flowing from her eyes in course of time, and congealed upon her cheeks, Master John her confessor, gently moistening with her other common tears, had carefully scraped off, and diligently storing them in a bag had kept by him in a clean casket.

CHAPTER XXVIII

OF THE WONDERFUL BEAUTY AND ASPECT OF HER COUNTENANCE

Now the virgin of exceeding humility had said that she would die like other men with very great sufferings, and that no miracles would happen at her death, which also befell as has already appeared. But nevertheless, lest God should seem altogether unmindful of the pain and toil of His poor and humble handmaid, and her praiseworthy patience be taken from the mouth of men, He also showed by undoubted signs before the sight of men with how great merits shone in Heaven the noble jewel long lying in the prison of the flesh. For her maiden face, which shunned the sight of men to behold more clearly the heavenly Spouse, presented no pallor or horror of death; but as if it had been anointed with oil or some aromatic liquor, shone with so great a brightness and becoming whiteness that it seemed to the beholders not as the common face of a mortal man or of a dead corpse, but as the likeness of a man glorified.

For those who were present said that they had never seen so beautiful a picture. Whence also, although many often approached to see her several times they could never see her enough. Likewise also the whole body shone with the same whiteness and a similar brilliancy, and all her members were resplendent with such a flush of health and beseeming fleshiness, as if she had never suffered any infirmity. The cleft also of her forehead seen formerly during life utterly vanished; the feet likewise and the legs, the hands and arms, and the neck appeared corpulent, and the whole body as entire as if there had never been any injury or wound therein before, except only that in the wound of her right arm, and in one wound inflicted upon her by the men of Picardy, small scars like a thread appeared in sign of the striking. Now the aforesaid Master John had three sisters german, who, when with other respectable matrons they watched by this venerable body, were filled with such grace by the sight and presence thereof that the whole time, to wit, from her passing to her burial, they were troubled by neither hunger, nor thirst, nor sleepiness.

ST. LYDWINE *of* SCHIEDAM

CHAPTER XXIX

OF THE FLOCKING OF VISITORS TO HER DEAD BODY

But her death being known, and the report of the glory of her body flying far and wide, so great a concourse of men flowed to visit her even to midnight, all the days that she remained unburied, that from the different states and towns of Rotterdam, of Delft, of Leyden, and Briel, and from other neighbouring towns and districts, so many hastened to the sight of this body that their certain number beyond many thousands cannot be assigned nor easily expressed. For children of three or four years, as if accustomed to walking, hastened with such eagerness that they urged even men of adult age to visit such great relics. Then the virgin could say if she had lived, "Suffer the little children to come unto me, for of such is the kingdom of Heaven" (Mark x 14). Having entered then the house in which was the holy bier, and because as children they were of small stature and could not lift themselves up to see the body in the place where it lay, many of them crying and grieving said: "Shall I not see this virgin, for whom I have come from so far?" Then the bystanders raised them up to see the face of the virgin, and after the sight sent them back to their homes with an alms of white bread. And what is more wonderful, there was also there a matron with a baby of one year and three months, which infant indeed, with joined hands and face turned towards the coffin, fixed his eyes so reverently and gravely thereon that the watchers and assistants of the sacred remains seeing and wondering at the infant's devotion were moved to tears.

CHAPTER XXX

OF THE STAINS WHICH SHE CONTRACTED FROM UNCLEAN MEN

On account of the most brave endurance of her sufferings, and her frequent familiarity with angels and conversation in Heaven, this virgin had arrived at such purity that, touched on the hand by unworthy and unclean men while still living, she sometimes visibly contracted stains, of which black marks remained on her hands two or three days, which had not been seen there before. So also after her death something of the like happened. For when her face after her death shone as has been said with such brilliancy, a certain matron came with others to visit, and passed her beads which she held in her hand over her face out of devotion as she thought, and immediately afterwards the maiden face from that contact was noticeably darkened. Wherefore, when her body had been placed in the church and some of the bystanders asked that it should be shown and the coffin opened for them, the rest, who knew of this darkening, absolutely forbade this to be done, fearing lest if it should be further darkened by the onlooking of the unworthy, others might be scandalised thence.

CHAPTER XXXI

OF HER REVERENTIAL BURIAL

At length on the Friday within the octave of Easter, which was the fourth day after her happy passing from this vale of tears and from the enclosure of the earthly dwelling, after the sacrifice of the Mass had been most devoutly celebrated she was given to burial, at the twelfth hour at midday, the sun shining brightly, and the day declining to its close, after the example of Christ, Who suffered on a Friday, died at the ninth hour, and was buried before sunset. To celebrate whose funeral rites was present the religious father Judocus, Prior of the Regulars of Briel, who had very often familiarly conversed with her in life, and had wisely tested many of the secrets of her sanctity. He persuaded for the better, and urged the people to suffer the servant of God to be buried in a Christian fashion. And when he had spoken the popular devotion agreed with the Prior, and at once her coffin, having been strongly fastened, the body of the holy virgin was given to burial after the example of Christ buried in the bosom of the earth, to be again raised by Him on the last day and glorified with all the saints in everlasting blessedness. And she was buried the beloved spouse of Christ,

ST. LYDWINE *of* SCHIEDAM

Lydia, white in virginity, deep in humility, perfected in patience, burning in charity, merciful, kind, excelling in devotion, sublime in contemplation, richly adorned with all the virtues and gifts of the Holy Ghost: not wrapt in silks, not enclosed in a marble tomb, but in a grave of stones befittingly formed with cement work; not in a royal city, but in her native town called Schiedam; not in a choir of clerics nor in a sanctuary of priests, but in the common cemetery of the parochial church of St. John Baptist, to the east of the temple, where the grave of the virgin may be seen and visited by all the inhabitants: not, however, deep in the earth nor covered above with earth, nor lifted high above the earth, but on beams of wood laid across within a stone grave. And this indeed very fittingly, that as for thirty years she had not touched the earth in life, so the earth should not touch her in death nor a mound of earth cover the casket of her body. Over whom is placed a large stone of red colour, beseemingly adorned within with divers red crosses, raised about two cubits above the mound of the grave.

CHAPTER XXXII

OF THE MIRACLES AFTER HER DEATH

After the burial of the venerable virgin, as many faithful visited her grave and honoured it with free offerings who asserted that they had been cured of various sicknesses and diseases the rulers of the city and the authorities of the church, having conceived a most praiseworthy design for the increase of the honour of God, the year following had built a stone chapel with an altar near her grave, about the feast of the ten thousand Martyrs,[1] to the praise and glory of God and the special memory of the same virgin, in the year of the Lord 1434.

CHAPTER XXXIII

THE NARRATION OF THREE MIRACLES

But now to prove this virgin's holiness it seems altogether befitting at the end of the book to adjoin, to the honour of

[1] June 22nd.

God and the praise of this holy virgin, of many signs three most notable miracles recently wrought by the co-operation of God, which are proved on the faith of worthy men testifying to her sanctity, and are reported by the lips of many.

FIRST MIRACLE

There was in the city of Delft a certain maiden who, continually keeping her bed for eight years, was grievously sick. This maiden four masters skilled in medicine and famous of repute visited, and moved by human pity, but urged more by the love of God, then strove to aid her. But the illness of this virgin was altogether unknown to these now mentioned masters, nor could any one of them give a remedy which might profit the sick girl. Among whom one of the masters, Master William Sonderdank, an approved doctor, wondering much, said to the above named maiden: "Thou hast not yet suffered so long a time such great pains as that blessed virgin Lydwine, because of whose merits the Lord now works many miracles in our parts." The sick virgin then hearing this, of her own devotion, or rather urged

ST. LYDWINE *of* SCHIEDAM

by divine inspiration, recited as many times the Lord's Prayer, commonly called the Our Father, as there are members in the human body, to the honour of God and this holy virgin Lydwine. It befell therefore after this that the happy virgin Lydwine visibly visited the sick maiden, giving her a remedy of medical art, and truly healed, she arose sound, walking, eating, and doing the works of maids in health. Whereat the aforesaid master, very much astounded, testifies that this is most true.

SECOND MIRACLE

The second miracle happened at Gouda, a most noted city of Holland. There was there in a cloister of virgins a certain nun who had a contraction of the nerves in one leg; which leg was so bent and shrunken that she could not walk, nor stretch it in any way to the length of the other by a space of two palms. She would willingly have visited this doctor Master William Sonderdank abovenamed, who before had cured one of the same house, sent to him in Delft, with the remedies of his art and the help of the grace of God in the space of eight weeks, but she could not obtain permission from her superiors. Saddened therefore, she wept bitterly several days, because she would remain lame all the days of her life, as she thought, ill content to be thus. At length came that blessed virgin Lydwine of a night speaking with her, and saying that she should ask of the sisters that every nun of that house should recite five Our Fathers and Hail Marys to the honour of God and the virgin Lydwine herself; and on the Sunday should have herself carried to her own church, and thus she should recover the health of the lame leg. Which was done without delay. For, having obtained leave of her confessor, she was carried to the church as Lydwine had said to her by vision, and during Mass she suddenly obtained the perfect cure of her leg; going out most joyously by herself, and rendering the greatest thanks to God, Who had worked that miracle by the merits of the most happy virgin Lydwine.

THIRD MIRACLE

But the third miracle happened at Leyden, a well-known town of the country of Holland. In this populous city there was a certain religious virgin who had in the neck a hard cancer about the size of a large apple, so that she could neither drink nor eat nor bend herself, if she did not wish to be choked by the exceeding difficulty of breathing. She came without shoes and without linen [1] to the grave of the aforesaid holy virgin to implore the succour of health, and not having gained it she returned with great sadness, not knowing what good things were to come to her. The night following after her return from the tomb, and awakened from her sleep, she was entirely cured of that cancerous growth which she had suffered for nearly eight years, as was known to many. This virgin miraculously cured the above mentioned Master William Sonderdank, doctor in medicine, saw with his own eyes and touched her neck with his hands; who also gives most trustworthy witness in his writing of all the foregoing, saying: "I witness to God that these three have been wrought within a short time; yea and many others which I have seen with my own eyes it would be too

[1] *i.e.* with only the rough outer garment against the skin by way of penance.

long to narrate."[1] These above written miracles have come to pass by God renewing wonders in our days, in the year of the Lord one thousand four hundred forty-eight, the most holy Pope Nicholas the Fifth sitting in the apostolic See, in the second year of his reign.

PRAISE TO GOD ALMIGHTY.

---

[1] This William Sonderdank was the son of the Godfrey of Hague, the Doctor who was the first to recognise the supernatural nature of Lydwine's ailments. This good Godfrey was accustomed to heal the poor *gratis*, and in response to their earnest *Grootendank*, Great thanks, he invariably answered *Sonderdank*, No thanks. Hence he was commonly known as Sonderdank, a title which his son was proud to take as a surname. This son, William, is also said to have built a hospital on the site of St. Lydwine's house, in accordance with the wish which she had once expressed when refusing the offer of a better house for herself: she had said that she would be well content if after her death her house should be fitted up as an asylum for the sick.

Printed in Great Britain
by Amazon